For ~~Xaa~~

You are raising a brilliant child !

Nurturing Brilliance:

Discovering and Developing Your Child's Gifts

by
Janine Walker Caffrey, Ed.D.

Great Potential Press™

Nurturing Brilliance: Discovering and Developing Your Child's Gifts

Edited by: Jennifer Ault
Interior design: The Printed Page
Cover design: Hutchison-Frey

Published by Great Potential Press, Inc.
7025 E. 1st Avenue, Suite 5
Scottsdale, AZ 85251

15 14 13 12 11   5 4 3 2 1

At the time of this book's publication, all facts and figures cited are the most current available. All telephone numbers, addresses, and website URLs are accurate and active; all publications, organizations, websites, and other resources exist as described in this book; and all have been verified as of the time this book went to press. The author(s) and Great Potential Press make no warranty or guarantee concerning the information and materials given out by organizations or content found at websites, and we are not responsible for any changes that occur after this book's publication. If you find an error or believe that a resource listed here is not as described, please contact Great Potential Press.

Library of Congress Cataloging-in-Publication Data

Caffrey, Janine Walker.
  Nurturing brilliance : discovering and developing your child's gifts / by Janine Walker Caffrey.
    p. cm.
  Includes bibliographical references and index.
  ISBN-13: 978-1-935067-12-2
  ISBN-10: 1-935067-12-5
1. Gifted children--Education. 2. Education--Parent participation. 3. Achievement motivation in children. I. Title.
  LC3993.C27 2011
  371.95--dc23
                    2011029393

To my parents, Adele and Howard Walker,
who discovered and developed the brilliance in all of their girls.

Table of Contents

Acknowledgments

This book was inspired by many brilliant children who were not aware that anyone was watching. Some were able to find their way, while others were not. Some had parents, teachers, and mentors who marveled at their brilliance, while others were simply misunderstood. I have been fortunate to know them and learn from them. Included in this group are my own children, Daniel the Storyteller and Alison the Melody Maker. This book contains their stories.

When this book was just an idea, my dear friend and agent Wendy Keller helped me bring it to life and encouraged me, even when it appeared that all was lost. I thank her for her unyielding loyalty and belief in me and my work.

As always, I thank my husband Drew for listening when everyone else was tired of hearing me talk, for reading when nobody else had the patience, and for telling me the truth when nobody else would dare.

Finally, I thank James Webb, Ph.D., Janet Gore, Jen Ault, and all of the wonderful people at Great Potential Press. They have dedicated their lives to brilliant children and have been amazing partners in the creation of this book. I thank them for pushing me to do my best work and for giving me a publishing home.

CHAPTER 1

Brilliance and How Our Children Shine

In a very typical kindergarten classroom, in a very typical public school, there was a little girl who was far from typical. She flitted around the room as if she were a teacher, approaching every other child as someone she needed to instruct and assist. The classroom was set up in learning centers, where students could practice their skills in letter recognition, counting, creative play, and the other business of five-year-olds. In each center, three or four students were focused and busy, clearly enjoying all that kindergarten had to offer. But this child was different. She was not content just to recognize the letters. She wanted to teach others about each letter and proceeded to do all she could to instruct them. Once she felt she had imparted the appropriate amount of knowledge, she went on to the "cooking" area, where several children were playing with the pretend kitchen items, making imaginary cuisine. Again, she felt compelled to instruct, giving them suggestions for other types of food that might please their pretend palates of the day. Alison seemed much more active than the other kids, yet she wasn't a hyperactive child. She was absolutely drawn to other children and seemed to yearn to make learning more exciting in their elementary world.

As I watched her, I became concerned because she did not seem to fit in with the others. She couldn't maintain focus for more than a minute or two in each area. Could she have an attention problem? Was there an emotional issue that prevented her from connecting with the others in a "normal" way? Just as my mind was racing with these thoughts, the teacher came up to me and said, "You know, Alison is always like this. She is different." This was so difficult for me to understand. At home she seemed so normal. Yet here at school, she was odd, out-of-step with the others. Was this good or bad? Should I be excited or terrified?

Not long after my impromptu visit to my daughter's class, I learned that the school wanted to conduct psychological testing on her to determine if she was "gifted." Alison's older brother was in second grade and was taking advantage of an accelerated class. He had been offered this class because the school had determined that he was "gifted." But Alison was nothing like Daniel. Daniel had begun talking at just six months old and was communicating in complete sentences before the age of one. We had always known that he had special skills in language. This became very apparent the summer between first and second grades, when he transitioned directly from reading Dr. Seuss to J.R.R. Tolkien. He actually finished reading *The Hobbit* before beginning second grade—it was the first chapter book he ever read!

However, unlike Alison, Daniel seemed like a normal kid in class. He was a typical boy who enjoyed playing with Transformers, digging for dinosaur bones, and tormenting his little sister. What I learned later is that many children exhibit different kinds of brilliance—they shine in different areas. One child may be brilliant in reading and writing but not have adequate skills in math. Another child may not excel at schoolwork at all yet be an amazing musician or athlete. As my own children grew, I became fascinated with all children who are particularly brilliant in particular areas. What makes them so good at one thing but simply average at another? Are there common traits across all areas of brilliance? Is there a relationship among various areas of brilliance? How can a child's brilliance best be nurtured and used to create a positive, extraordinary life?

It is essential that parents and educators truly understand who these gifted children are and what they need. The first step in this process is to define brilliance.

Definitions

So how do we define brilliance? Our federal government defines "gifted and talented" as "Students, children, or youth who give evidence of high achievement capability in areas such as intellectual, creative, artistic, or leadership capacity, or in specific academic fields, and who need services and activities not ordinarily provided by the school in order to fully develop those capabilities."[1] The National Association for Gifted Children (NAGC) has developed a new and broader definition:[2]

> *Gifted individuals are those who demonstrate outstanding levels of aptitude (defined as an exceptional ability to reason and learn) or competence (documented performance or achievement in top 10% or rarer) in one or more domains. Domains include any structured area of activity with its own symbol system (e.g., mathematics, music, language) and/or set of sensorimotor skills (e.g., painting, dance, sports).*
>
> *The development of ability or talent is a lifelong process. It can be evident in young children as exceptional performance on tests and/or other measures of ability or as a rapid rate of learning, compared to other students of the same age, or in actual achievement in a domain. As individuals mature through childhood to adolescence, however, achievement and high levels of motivation in the domain become the primary characteristics of their giftedness. Various factors can either enhance or inhibit the development and expression of abilities.*

Many people believe that you know giftedness when you see it, but I am not so sure. I have been around many children with hidden talents and abilities that, once uncovered, open the door to their true potential. We don't always see these gifts and talents because, although official definitions include a wide range of characteristics, in reality, we typically only recognize a traditional IQ model and those children of high ability who are achieving academically, not the underachieving ones. Consider Howard Gardner's take on this topic.

Gardner is a psychologist and researcher who developed a theory of intelligence, built on the work of others before him, that he described in his book *Frames of Mind: The Theory of Multiple Intelligences*.[3] He coined the phrase "multiple intelligences" and went on to describe a completely fresh definition of intelligence. Gardner believes that all human beings have minds with multiple traits in eight areas:

- ✔ Linguistic Intelligence
- ✔ Logical-Mathematical Intelligence
- ✔ Musical Intelligence
- ✔ Spatial Intelligence
- ✔ Bodily-Kinesthetic Intelligence
- ✔ Interpersonal Intelligence
- ✔ Intrapersonal Intelligence
- ✔ Naturalist Intelligence

Frames of Mind was a groundbreaking book because it celebrated a variety of strengths that humans exhibit, allowing us to see our abilities in many areas, not just traditional academic ones. Parents and educators who study Gardner's work are able to assist children in learning as they learn best, experiencing a much richer education as a result. While Gardner's theories have done much to broaden our view of intelligence, we can do still more. We need to redefine brilliance into a simple framework, focusing on using children's passions to fuel their development and lead them to fulfilling and perhaps extraordinary lives.

Redefining "Gifted"

The term "gifted" has come to mean a variety of things to a variety of people. In order to shatter earlier stereotypes and provide a working description of these extraordinary children, I will cease using the word "gifted" for the remainder of this book and replace it with the word "brilliant." In my opinion, this word is much better suited to describe children who have abilities and talents that immediately garner (or should garner) the attention of those around them.[4] These are kids who are different from the rest and who often, but not always, stand out. We want to watch them and engage with them in a different way than with other children. Their abilities make them capable of extraordinary lives. It is our job to assist them in discovering and developing their brilliance.

A brilliant child is one who shines in a unique way in one or multiple disciplines of language, math, science, leadership, art, music, dance, performance, and athletics. Most of these children exhibit brilliance in more than one discipline, but they really shine in one particular area. Generally that is the area that needs to be nurtured the most because the child will have the motivation to achieve and succeed and follow his own passions there more than in any other area.

There are two common threads that I have noticed among all brilliant children, regardless of their area(s) of brilliance. First, brilliant children frequently make connections better than other children. For example, they somehow see a link between musical and scientific concepts, or they understand innately the impact of a famous literary figure on the leadership abilities of a current politician. The second thing that all brilliant children seem to have in common is a finely honed sense of humor, which can show itself in a variety of settings and often in unexpected ways.

Areas of Brilliance

Every bright child has a tendency toward certain areas of brilliance, but most tend to really shine in one predominant area.

Storytellers are those people who love language. They generally talk at a very young age, learn to read easily, and enjoy expressing themselves through speaking and writing. *Calculators* see the world through patterns, numbers, and equations. They are highly logical thinkers who enjoy creating order in the world. Those who like to discover things are *Explorers*. They like to figure things out through experimentation and, when nurtured properly, can grow up to cure diseases and create innovative technology. Great leaders in politics, business, and other pursuits are usually *Magnets*. People will follow them anywhere and rally around them for a good cause. *Designers* see the world as one giant canvas. They like to make everything more beautiful or use images to make the rest of us think. They are usually quiet artists with deep thoughts and strong feelings. For *Melody Makers*, life is one big song. They hear melodies and rhythms in everything that happens around them. They enjoy hearing unusual sounds and making music everywhere they go. Our graceful *Butterflies* jump and leap and pirouette through the world. They experience life with their whole bodies and express themselves with dance and movement. For *Charmers*, all the world is a stage. They believe that we all should be watching them and command us to do so with every word and deed. We don't mind; we usually can't keep our eyes off of them because they are so fascinating to watch. *Warriors* enjoy physical activities and athletic events involving tough competition and high adrenaline. They are fearless and like to physically push themselves further than we think they can go.

It is critical for parents and educators to understand children who have tendencies toward brilliance in a particular area. Only then can we know what motivates them.

Sparks

Once you understand what type of child you have been blessed with, you can really have some fun. A spark is an activity or experience that gets a child's passions engaged, and it is the first step in nurturing brilliance. As you can imagine, different things are interesting to different kinds of children. As a parent, you must be tireless in your efforts to continually engage your child in his or her area of brilliance.

My son Daniel is a Storyteller to the extreme. He knew he wanted to write for a living from the time he knew what a writer was. His main interest as a young teen was film. The summer he turned 13, a new video rental store opened up within biking distance of our house. Daniel was so excited that he convinced his father to sign for him to be able to rent R-rated movies. I was against it, fearing that he would watch too much violence or sex and be ruined for life. But my husband explained to me that Daniel had discussed with him how he wanted to study the films and was particularly interested in gangster flicks like *Goodfellas* and *The Godfather*. Daniel could enhance his skills as a writer if he could go independently to the store to research and select the films of interest to him. Trusting my husband's parenting instincts (which are usually right), I reluctantly agreed.

What happened that summer truly amazed me. Every night at dinner, it was as if we were in a graduate film studies class. Daniel and his father dissected each film, discussing plot elements, special effects, character motivation, the screen writer's intentions, and everything else you might or might not want to know about the gangster genre. Most of the time I had absolutely no idea what they were talking about.

That "Blockbuster summer" was a spark for Daniel—something that motivated him and helped him shine. Every child needs sparks. It is up to parents to think of fun ways to encourage their children to develop their areas of brilliance and inspire them to accomplish great things.

Education

Our schools could play an excellent role in finding the sparks that help brilliant children realize their potential. In fact, the Elementary and Secondary Education Act of 2002 provides a comprehensive definition that covers all areas of brilliance and seems to allow states and school districts to fund wonderful resources for these amazing kids. This means that children who need something different educationally due to the potential of high achievement can be considered "gifted" and can be eligible for these extra resources that will stimulate their learning and get them excited and motivated to achieve in school. Can you imagine a school system that truly provides what each individual child needs?

But that is not how it works. As schools struggle with budget shortfalls and unfunded mandates, many programs and resources that would truly benefit brilliant children are cut. Although each state and/or school district has a process to identify eligible students and enroll them in appropriate programs, and despite the fact that the original intent of these processes was to find students who need and could benefit from gifted education, in reality, many practices have the unintended effect of weeding out students whose parents are just not savvy enough to work the system. For example, some school districts require that students register for testing by a certain date. If parents miss the deadline, they have to wait an additional year. Other school districts may depend on teachers to recommend a student for testing by completing a brief survey or questionnaire, but parents may not be aware that they must ask the teacher to take this action. In order to ensure that a child receives consideration for programs, parents must learn what process is required and initiate action when appropriate.

Further, some educators are biased against programs for advanced learners and simply refuse to refer children for testing. When my daughter was clearly demonstrating that she needed more challenge and was extremely frustrated in her elementary class, her teacher would not submit the required behavioral checklist and achievement testing for a teacher referral. She told me that she believed that Alison did not meet the standard and that, in fact, she did not agree with having those kinds of programs at all. Fortunately, I understood that I, as a parent, had the right to challenge this, and I did. Alison was finally tested and admitted to the program based on a single IQ score that was well above the required mark.

In New York City, to avoid this type of teacher bias, the administration has established an open test that can be taken by *any* child during a set period of time each year. Students, generally at the age of four, are referred by their parents. Each parent completes a form and signs up for a testing date. In the weeks leading up to the test, many parents take their children to individual coaches and tutors to prep for the test. Unfortunately, this has resulted in programs that are much more likely to cater to students of certain socio-economic brackets who may or may not be appropriately placed in classes and programs for advanced learners.

In addition, school districts often exclude children with the slightest hint of a behavioral issue from appropriate programs. Ironically, putting a child in the gifted program will in many cases alleviate the behavioral issue.

School should be fun and enjoyable, especially for brilliant children. When school is working well, children are excited to go, and they look forward to upcoming events. It is easy to know when a child's education is not working, though. The child will become disobedient or will begin to dislike school. Watch for signs of poor behavior or boredom so that you can address them with the child's teacher or school. Sometimes a change in curriculum is helpful. Perhaps the child needs a more accelerated reading or math class. Other times a particular teacher may be problematic, while a different teacher can be inspiring.

As a parent, you can also explore elective classes, clubs, or sports to rekindle a dying flame of interest in your brilliant child. If none of these things works, it may be time to consider a different school or an alternative educational environment, such as an online program, a professional school for children, or even homeschooling. When your child is not thriving in school, it is vital that you learn as much as possible about her strengths and weaker areas, as well as the various options available in order to advocate successfully for her education. Parents should consult the wide variety of resources available on this topic.[5]

The Bane of Brilliance

There are many factors that prevent brilliant children from getting what they need to feel safe, accomplished, and happy. If we don't address these issues, our children may be at risk for a life of misery and lost potential. Brilliance is often misunderstood and is frequently misjudged. Many people think these kids are so smart that they can make it on their own, without any special help or guidance. But brilliant children are still children, and they need adults to lead them down the paths of discovery, encouraging them and assisting them in finding the resources they need to grow and develop their talents. I once overheard a cafeteria worker interacting with a group of children from the gifted elementary school class. She was frustrated because the children were excessively noisy and silly while waiting in line for their lunches. She said, "You guys are gifted! You should behave properly!"—to which one of the students retorted, "Just because we're smart doesn't mean we behave better."

Sometimes children who are labeled "gifted" become objects of inappropriate expectations or even ridicule. "Gifted education" has become a derogatory term to describe programs that many wish did not exist. They may be seen as elitist, particularly if they focus only on the upper 2% or 3% of students. One prominent educator in my community, when approached about improving programs for gifted children, smugly remarked, "Oh great—more perks for the privileged," even though a brilliant child is just as likely to come from a background that is not so privileged.

Although many people assume that brilliant children have a higher rate of academic success than average-ability children, many of them underachieve and actually drop out of high school entirely.[6] Accurate statistics in this area are difficult to determine, but what we do know is that young people with high levels of intellect, as measured by IQ tests and participation in Advanced Placement courses, represent up to 20% of those who leave high school prematurely.[7] For many, the tedium of boring classes and a lock-step curriculum that leaves no room for exploration in their areas of brilliance is too much to bear, and once they are of an age at which they can get away from this environment—despite the potential consequences for their future prospects—they do.

What about the brilliant kids who don't drop out? The high IQ scores of these advanced learners might suggest that these individuals will go on to have extraordinary careers and demonstrate great leadership. But this does not seem to be the case either. "In terms of professional achievement, …the men as well as the women [in one study] seemed to gain some margin of benefit from the extra IQ points, although neither group has produced a record of uniformly outstanding achievement. Indeed, the overall impression is one of lower achievement than the traditional view of IQ would have predicted for both groups."[8] In fact, the careers of high-IQ individuals are most likely to top off at the middle management level in traditional business structures. Contrary to what we might expect, brilliant children usually do not turn into our leaders of tomorrow—at least, not without the proper nurturing to help them develop their abilities into gifts that they can be proud of.

As you can see, contrary to what many people believe, brilliant children are at risk for underachievement and loss of potential when the adults in their lives make assumptions about them concerning their abilities. Brilliant kids *do* have problems, just like other children. They need to be guided and coached, just like other children. They need opportunities to stretch their minds and engage their talents, just like other children, although parents and educators cannot do this in the same way that they challenge and engage other children. But brilliant children also have differences that create additional challenges for them, beyond what most average-ability children experience.

Relationships

Friends are a powerful influence in every child's life. But finding friends and developing relationships can sometimes be more challenging for a brilliant child, who may seem out of step with the rest of the world. You want your child to find a peer group to cheer her on and encourage her gifts. Unfortunately, many kids can be cruel to others who are different from them. They may become jealous or feel threatened by another child's brilliance and tease or bully the child about the very gifts that make her special. Finding kindred spirits may be difficult when so few can relate to the brilliant child's advanced thinking or abilities. However, when these children do find like-minded peers, the friendships can become deeply intense.

This concept becomes even more critical as the child moves through adolescence and young adulthood and seeks romantic companionship. These incredibly powerful relationships can be intensely rewarding or emotionally devastating for a brilliant person. You must keep an open line of communication with your child so that if relationship issues become difficult for her, you can gently offer a more mature, objective perspective that can help her deal with her feelings in an appropriate manner.

Because of the difficulty that brilliant children often have with finding intellectual peers, many of them tend to feel more comfortable with older children or adults who share their gifts. As an example, I had the pleasure recently of seeing a popular band perform, and I was able to spend time with the musicians at the end of the show, one of whom was only 15 years old! I asked her if she missed her high school friends at home and how it felt to be on the road with a group of people in their late 20s and early 30s. She explained that although she has some good friends her own age, they just don't understand her devotion to her music. She went on to describe how satisfying it is for her to be challenged by other artists who are as talented as she. Overall, she enjoys a life that is balanced with "normal" teen experiences and incredible music experiences that allow her to grow as a musician and performer. You can help your brilliant child by allowing her to walk in both worlds.

Asynchronous Development

A characteristic common to brilliant individuals is their asynchrony, which is their unevenness in development. There are actually two different ways in which brilliant children can be asynchronous. The first is related to their development as compared to others around them. They are frequently out of step with their age peers, who generally approach developmental milestones at approximately the same time as one another. Brilliant children who are advanced in one or more areas hit some of these milestones much sooner than other children, and so they often find that they are different and don't fit in well with classmates and play groups of children who are the same age as they. This is one of the reasons why forming friendships and romantic relationships can be so difficult for them.

The other way in which brilliant children can be asynchronous is within themselves. Some of these individuals are well-rounded and can function very well in the world because of their multiple abilities. However, many brilliant people have one very strong aspect of their brain, body, or personality that enables them to compensate for other areas that are weaker or underdeveloped. For example, a Calculator with tremendous logical ability, memory, and number sense may have difficulty, or even a learning disability, in the area of reading. This person may use his memory and logic to his advantage, simply remembering things and deducing, and avoiding reading at all costs.

Due to this tendency toward "unevenness," many brilliant children and adults are out of balance. Their brains seem to become wired in only one direction, making it difficult for them to accomplish things in other areas. You will need to use your child's strengths and interests to assist him in learning other things that are important. After all, a Calculator's math and logic skills will not get him very far if he can't read! You want to strike just the right balance of encouragement and insistence to remedy this problem. Remediation or tutoring may be necessary.

When brilliant children display asynchrony, whether by being different from their peers or by demonstrating strength in one area and then struggling to maintain that high level of ability in all subjects, it oftentimes highlights to them just how different they are from their classmates and the others around them. These children need adults to help them understand themselves and accept themselves for who they are, in all their strengths and weaknesses. When they know that there is not something wrong with them just because they learn faster or differently, or just because they aren't brilliant at everything, they can learn to feel good about themselves and appreciate their abilities as gifts to be nurtured and enjoyed.

Mental Health

When one considers that brilliant children are frequently struggling with inappropriate classroom experiences, finding like-minded friends who understand and appreciate them, fitting in with their age peers, and understanding (and perhaps remediating) their uneven development, it should not be surprising that these children can experience emotional difficulties. However, many people make the assumption that high levels of ability should enable young people to avoid experiencing emotional problems. In reality, these children are no more or less likely to suffer from mental illness than their average-ability peers. However, there is research that notes a higher occurrence of some mood disorders (i.e., bipolar, depression) and suicide among highly creative individuals.[9]

Children with advanced abilities, and the adults they become, are more prone to engage in a great deal of questioning about the meaning of life, and they may be more likely to develop existential depression as a result.[10] They also tend to be very sensitive and quite intense, exhibiting reactions and behaviors that may become problematic. For example, they are often strong-willed, may overreact emotionally to minor situations, and tend to be overly idealistic and perfectionistic.[11]

These tendencies for brilliant children to seem extreme in their reactions to the world around them can lead adults to misdiagnose them with problems that they do not actually have. Misdiagnosis of mental illness poses a particular problem for them. When presented with talented learners who exhibit behaviors and tendencies that are related to their advanced abilities, some caregivers are quick to diagnose conditions such as Attention Deficit Hyperactivity Disorder, Bipolar Disorder, Obsessive-Compulsive Disorder, Oppositional-Defiant Disorder, or even depression. This puts these children at risk of receiving powerful drugs that they do not need and which may cause them harm.[12]

Sometimes what can appear as unusual behavior is actually quite typical for a brilliant child. Other times, what parents may believe is normal for a brilliant child may actually be a sign of a problem. Parents of brilliant children sometimes have difficulty discerning between high energy and hyperactivity, moodiness and depression. These children can often seem extreme in their behaviors and moods.

So how do you know when you need to worry? Who can help you when there is a problem? It is critical to have a full understanding of what constitutes quirks and what can be real issues that need to be addressed in brilliant children. In addition to causing these children to lose potential, mental health issues can be extremely dangerous. Every parent needs to understand this important aspect of the human condition. If this issue is of particular concern for you, there are wonderful resources that can be helpful.[13]

Help Your Brilliant Child Shine

You can make a positive impact in all of these issues. Through relatively simple, fun strategies outlined in this book, your child can grow to lead a truly extraordinary life. Read on to learn how you can help your brilliant child shine!

CHAPTER 2

Illumination: Identifying Your Child's Area of Brilliance

Most children have one special area where their brilliance is most apparent—where it really shines. Although a child may have abilities in multiple areas, there is usually one in which the child has a strong, compelling interest and to which he or she feels drawn like a moth to a flame.

Storytellers

I really can't remember when my son Daniel wasn't talking. It seemed he came out of the womb with his language skills already developed. Daniel was a calm baby, but he had an insatiable need for interaction. He made eye contact the day he was born and seemed to engage us in communication immediately. I could not leave him for a second as an infant. He wanted me to talk with him and interact with him constantly. So the housework and everything else waited. By the time he was about six months old, he was talking. Some of his first words were "trash truck." He loved trucks and could identify each specific type of truck that he had seen in

The Big Book of Trucks when he saw it in the real world. If he saw a truck that wasn't in that book, he would ask what it was. I have to admit, I made up a few names because I had no idea what some of the trucks were really called, and in the pre-Internet days of the 1980s, I had to provide very quick answers to my inquisitive child, still months shy of his first birthday.

I guess I didn't realize just how exceptional Daniel's abilities were until I looked back at some video of him years later. He was my first baby, and I was a special education teacher, so my frame of reference was with disabled children. I figured that he was just what "normal" looked like. But when Daniel was about five or six, I discovered an old video of him taken when he had been just six months old. In the video, we were visiting a friend. He was sitting in an infant seat on the kitchen table, and we were feeding him a jar of baby food. He was talking in sentences of three to four words. I played the tape over and over, suddenly realizing just how unusual Daniel's behavior was.

So I put in another tape of Daniel at his second birthday party. In this tape, he was rambling on about an antique train set that we had displayed in our home. He was describing in great detail the features of each car, what it was used for, etc. I remembered that conversation with Daniel after watching the tape. He had talked about that train for weeks. The conversation evolved into a discussion of the people who probably rode on trains like that and where they might be going. This was all around the time when he had just turned two!

Daniel's love of language continued throughout his childhood. He wanted us to read to him every day and night, beginning when he was just a few months old. By the time he was about a year old, he had memorized his favorite books as we read them, and he insisted that we read them over and over again. If we tried to skip anything in our efforts to get him to bed a little sooner, he would correct us and require that we add in the missing parts. He loved all kinds of books. He enjoyed the word play of Dr. Seuss just as much as intricate stories and nonfiction.

One day, toward the end of first grade, Daniel spotted my husband's illustrated copy of *The Hobbit* on a bookshelf. He asked if he could look at it, so I brought the book to him. He looked through it, intrigued by the illustrations. Then he boldly announced, "I am going to read this book." That didn't seem likely, and I imagined that we would end up reading it to him, but not wanting to discourage him, I responded, "Okay." Daniel started at the first page and just kept reading. Within a couple of weeks, he had finished the entire book and was enjoying discussions about it with my husband. This was during the summer between first and second grades!

Storytellers are those who love words and using them to communicate. They cannot quell their need to talk to others and want to engage in communication constantly. They typically read insatiably and at a level far advanced for their age group.

Is your child a Storyteller? Take a look at the questions below. If you can answer "yes" to at least three of them, you may have a budding Storyteller on your hands.

- ✔ Did your child talk at an early age? Did he say words earlier than 10 or 11 months of age and put them together to form ideas around 12 months or earlier?

- ✔ Did your child begin reading before anyone explicitly taught him to do so? Was he independently recognizing words before age four?

- ✔ Does your child have a vivid imagination? Does he frequently describe or act out what he is seeing in his mind's eye to others and draw them into his imagination?

- ✔ Does your child write out his stories or poems or songs and share them with others?

- ✔ Does your child have difficulty writing within the confines of school assignments or assessments, refusing to produce just what teachers expect in response to canned prompts?

Your Storyteller will enrich your home with lively conversations about in-depth topics of interest. Make sure that there are plenty of reading materials available in a wide variety of genres and subjects. Trips to the library and to bookstores should be regular outings for these budding wordsmiths.

Calculators

Maria discovered puzzles at about age three. She loved to fit the pieces together to create an image out of the seeming chaos of the individual pieces, and she was proud of her quick ability to do so. Later, when she was just a little older, she discovered Sudoku and learned that those kinds of puzzles could be solved with numbers. This was her introduction to math. Maria was attracted to mathematics because she understood the rules of math and enjoyed the constancy of it; although there can be new math challenges, she could use concepts she already knew to find the solutions. There may be multiple paths to those solutions, but in the end, the results will be the same. Math creates a world where things are predictable and safe, and Calculators love this world.

Maria also loved to organize things. She organized her hair barrettes by color, shape, and size. She frequently helped her mother in the kitchen by sorting through the utensils in the drawer and putting the plastic containers in order by size and purpose. When Maria describes events, she usually discusses them in concrete, sequential terms, rarely relating information about her feelings or aesthetic qualities of the environment.

Maria really loves school. She enjoys the structure and order of it, gladly adhering to the rules that keep things organized. But she does not always enjoy her math class. She resents it when the teacher requires her to practice things she has already mastered; she yearns for more complex problems to conquer and wants to be left on her own to solve them.

Calculators will work their way through life's difficulties by using organization and logic. "If this, then that…" statements form the foundation for their actions. Even when they are experiencing extreme emotions, they will use linear problem-solving techniques to get themselves back on track and moving through their predictable world again.

If you can answer "yes" to at least three of the following questions, you probably have a Calculator in your family.

- ✔ Does your child frequently organize things into categories?

- ✔ Does your child enjoy puzzles, particularly those involving numbers? Did she begin doing advanced puzzles earlier than most other children?

- ✔ Is your child comforted by order and rules? Does she seek to put them in place when they are absent?

- ✔ Does your child deal with emotions by using logic?

- ✔ Is your child able to solve complex math problems without writing down all of the steps? Is it sometimes difficult for her to explain how she arrived at the right answer because she just "knows it"?

Your Calculator will never cease to amaze you with her logic and advanced skills. Organization and structure will be important to her. However, be sure she gets all of the challenge she needs to continue to grow and learn.

Explorers

Anna has an insatiable desire to know "why." She asks this question continually, and she completely exhausts both of her parents in the process. If she wants to know how a small appliance works, she just takes it apart to figure it out. Anna loves nature, too, and sometimes puts herself at risk trying to understand things like the workings of a bee hive or how a tree is put together. She is constantly thinking, asking questions, and experimenting with things so she can better understand her world.

When Anna was only about three years old, she learned that a magnifying glass could be used to focus sunlight and make a dry leaf smoke. Luckily, her mother intervened before any damage was done! When Anna was four, she went through what her parents referred to as her "water year." For the entire year, she was obsessed with water and how it interacts with everything else. She set up elaborate contraptions to lead water from the wading pool to the garden, or from the bathroom sink to the toilet. She learned that the pressure of running water could push it upward, and that water ran faster if it was heading down toward the ground. She was fascinated by the ripples of water on the edge of the lake where they swam, and she dug different-shaped holes to see how she could capture the most. Anna's parents had to answer countless questions about water and help their preschooler surf the Internet to find more information. They took her to aquariums, bought books about water, and lived the year of water right alongside their inquisitive daughter. And then, just as suddenly as it started, Anna's interest in water stopped. One day, she simply seemed satisfied with her knowledge of water and moved on to insects, beginning what would come to be known as her "insect year."

You know when you are in the home of an Explorer because every gadget has been taken apart. They are sometimes put back together, but not always. These children are fascinated by how things work and have an insatiable appetite for discovery. They are continually experimenting just to see what will happen, and they don't really understand why people make such a fuss when the vacuum cleaner is found in pieces after one of their self-tutorials.

Explorers constantly ask "why" and are not satisfied with cursory responses. They have inquiring minds that need to know. It can be fatiguing to be the parent of an Explorer, who will push your thinking in ways that you cannot imagine. Some Explorers move from subject to subject, like Anna; others are never done learning about a particular topic. Most strive to learn everything there is to know about something that interests them.

Do you have an Explorer in your world? Here are some questions for you.

✔ Does your child take apart small appliances and gadgets?

✔ Does your child wander around outside and enjoy being in the midst of bugs, animals, and plants?

✔ Does your child constantly ask "why" and seem unsatisfied with your answers because they lack enough information?

✔ Does your child experiment with things, continually trying to understand "what might happen if"?

✔ Does your child perseverate on particular subjects for prolonged periods of time, seemingly trying to learn everything about the topic at hand?

If you answered "yes" to at least three of these questions, prepare to be exhausted. The life of the parent of an Explorer is one filled with endless questions, dismantled household objects, and never-ending conversations about topics of questionable interest. It is also filled with amazing experiments and fascinating explorations!

Magnets

When I was growing up, Mike was the king of our block. In the park, the neighborhood kids played a variety of games that had specific rules and procedures. When we had questions about them, we asked Mike. If we wanted to know just how much risk was wise, we watched Mike and did just a little bit less. He was a daredevil, a hard charger. I remember watching him fly down the street on his bike—usually with either his feet off the pedals or his hands in the air or both. He seemed to defy the rules when he wasn't making his own. We all wanted to be near him, to emulate him, to be with him. He drew us to him. When Mike talked, everybody listened. He seemed to have an innate sense of the world that the rest of us craved. We felt that if he was in control, we would know what to do and would be safe in the structure that he created. Today, Mike is a world-renowned motivational speaker and even appeared in a movie.

Mike is a Magnet. This quality is typically easy to spot in groups of children. Just check out a mass of students on the playground during unstructured recess. The Magnets are the kids who pick the sides for the kickball game when there is no teacher around. Look around the cafeteria. The Magnets are the ones who establish the social makeup of the lunch tables. Simply put, they are the ones in charge when the grown-ups are not. All of the other children want to be with them and strive to be like them.

There was a boy in my high school who was an amazing Magnet. He organized several overnight ski trips without any parental or teacher involvement. We all thought that these were school-sanctioned trips. They were not! In the days before computers or even photocopiers, this teen managed to get a hold of enough school letterhead to create official-looking school permission slips for all the kids who wanted to take part in the outings, and he arranged with a tour company to have tour busses pick us up at the school long before dawn. So large numbers of high school students went on non-school-sanctioned ski trips for three days at a time, with only one rather unscrupulous tour guide to chaperone. We never questioned this. We just took the fake permission forms to our parents, saved our babysitting and lawn mowing money, and went on the trips. Recently, when a group of us got together, we realized what this youngster, now a highly successful financial officer of a major corporation, had done. He had gotten everyone—children and adults alike—to follow him blindly in the creation and execution of unchaperoned overnight trips. He did it because he thought it would be great fun, and it really was. Luckily, nobody got hurt and all ended well.

Magnets have natural leadership ability that draws people to them and that influences the actions of those around them. Do you feel the pull of a magnetic child in your home? You probably do if you can answer "yes" to at least three of thee following questions.

- ✔ When your child is with a group of other children, do they tend to gather round him and listen to his every word?

- ✔ Does your child assume a leadership position when there are no adults around? For example, does he become the "captain" responsible for picking teams?

- ✔ Does your child seem to get away with things for which others might be punished?

✔ Does your child tend to make the rules for informal social groups of children?

✔ Is your child considered popular?

Magnets are natural leaders who can use their talents for the benefit of others, but they are also capable of hurting those around them through control and manipulation. Many business, political, and religious leaders are Magnets who are influential all around the world. However, these same individuals can sometimes drift into narcissism and poor judgment that result in harm to others—as well as sensational headlines. It is a great responsibility to raise a Magnet. Be sure that you provide him with a solid moral foundation so that he can use his talents to be a force for good in the world.

Designers

Terrell didn't really like school. He only wanted to draw. Everything he experienced became illustrated. While other children were playing with toys, he was creating clothes for his action figures and forming paper structures as their homes. He liked to use strings and ribbons to create unusual worlds in his bedroom or the living room. He was unhappy unless things were decorated and color-coordinated, and he insisted on being consulted on every purchase for the home. He often attempted to rearrange the furniture to make it more aesthetically pleasing, and he was appalled if his mother purchased something new for the kitchen that didn't fit into the color scheme. Terrell was also very particular about the clothes he wore. At the age of six, he decided that he needed to wear red every day, equating this color to his personality somehow. He said that he felt undressed unless this color was evident in his clothes daily. Terrell defined his world through colors and shapes and textures.

Terrell is a Designer—one who pays particular attention to how things look and go together in every way. Some Designers are not so obvious; they may not have opinions about home decorating or clothing. Instead, they are constantly creating visual images in their heads that find their way to paper or canvas. These children use pictures to convey ideas, are typically deep thinkers, and are often very intense but also very quiet.

The Designer is all about images, pictures, colors, and textures. It is difficult to get his attention for mundane tasks, particularly the academic kind. You have to appeal first to his sense of artistry in order to get him to learn the necessary skills one needs to function in the world.

Take a look at these questions and see if you might be parenting a Designer.

- ✔ Did your child begin drawing at an early age, forming shapes and figures before the age of four?

- ✔ Does your child take objects from nature and around the house to create new pieces of art at every opportunity?

- ✔ Is your child distracted by colors, shapes, and textures, sometimes focusing on a particular one to the exclusion of all others?

- ✔ Does your child use pictures or images instead of words to convey ideas or to make sense of the world?

- ✔ Does your child ignore academic requirements or home chores in favor of drawing, painting, or creating other types of art work?

If at least three of these points describe your child, you may be the proud parent of a budding Designer, ready to make the world a more beautiful place!

Melody Makers

Alison seemed to sing songs before she could talk. It didn't matter if she understood what the song lyrics meant; she sang them anyway. By the time she was three, she was singing multiple verses of many songs. And she was drawn to really good music. She asked that particular artists be played while we were in the car—but not what you would expect. Although the typical "kids'" music of the day was alright, she never requested it. Instead, she asked to hear the wonderful jazz stylings of Ella Fitzgerald or the old standards of Frank Sinatra. She enjoyed blues music that was her dad's favorite, following the predictable chord progressions with great intensity.

By the time Alison was about eight years old, she was eagerly trying every new musical instrument available to her. Without any real instruction, she could intuitively play anything. She impressed the music teacher at her school so much with her ability that she was allowed to join a chorus and band normally reserved for fifth graders when she was only in third grade!

While all children appreciate and enjoy music, Melody Makers create it whenever they can, wherever they are. These children need music in their lives more than anything else. They have a perpetual "soundtrack" playing in their heads at all times and need to be with others who share their musical sensibilities. Do you have a Melody Maker in your midst? Consider the following questions.

- ✔ Does your child have an innate sense of rhythm? Do you notice her moving to a beat even when there is no music playing?

- ✔ Does your child constantly sing, hum, or tap out the beat of songs?

- ✔ Did your child crave music at a very young age, asking you to sing or play music for her? Did her taste include lots of different types of music not typical for a child?

- ✔ Is your child able to play a musical instrument with little or no formal instruction? Does she just seem to know what to do with new instruments?

- ✔ Does your child hear music in familiar sounds in the environment, making music out of what others consider noise?

If you answered "yes" to three or more of these questions, your child may be a Melody Maker. How lucky you are to have someone who will fill your house with music!

Butterflies

Sumiko always seemed to float gracefully about her environment. Although she had no formal dance training, she had the posture of a dancer. She seemed to feel every subtle movement and was sensitive to her body in a way that was unusual for a sixth grader. At a time when most girls her age were trying to hide their physicality, Sumiko seemed to revel in hers. She held her head high and flitted like a butterfly. She never really walked anywhere; there was always a little flutter of the fingers or a pointing of the toes as she skipped, leapt, or jumped along. When she heard music—actual or the stuff in her head—she couldn't help but to move to it, dancing as though her movements had been carefully choreographed, even though they weren't.

By the time Sumiko was nearing the end of middle school, she caught the eye of the head of a local dance company and was asked to dance in their production of *The Nutcracker*. While most of the girls her age had small parts, Sumiko played the main role of Clara, much to the chagrin of the girls who had been in *The Nutcracker* since they were old enough to don a pair of ballet slippers. But Sumiko looked different than the other girls—naturally poised and balanced—and she exhibited great confidence, which was unfortunately sometimes interpreted as arrogance. She required perfection from herself and was not intimidated by the demanding dance teacher the way some of the other girls were. She knew that she was good, but she always wanted to be better. When Sumiko was in the dance studio, which she considered her second home, she was focused and intense, doing whatever it took to become the very best dancer she could be.

Butterflies are an amazing combination of physicality, design aesthetic, and musicianship. They move in ways that seem to defy gravity, creating incredible beauty in the world just by their presence. See if you might have a Butterfly child by answering the following questions.

✔ Does your child have unusually good posture and hold her head "just so" when she walks and moves?

✔ Do your child's movements seem almost choreographed, even when she is just making her way down a hallway?

✔ Does your child have long, willowy limbs that are graceful and seem to tell a story?

✔ Does your child like to be in constant motion but with grace and purpose?

✔ Does your child have an artistic sensibility, appreciating the details of beautiful things?

If you answered "yes" to at least three of these questions, you may be in the presence of a beautiful Butterfly.

Charmers

Alejandro craves the spotlight. Whenever there is a camera around, he is in front of it. If there is a group presentation to be made, he is the man for the job. He has a twinkle in his eye and a swagger in his step that seems to command all the world to take notice of him. Wherever he goes, heads turn and eyes light up. Everyone everywhere seems to want to look at him and drink him in.

When Alejandro entered first grade, the buzz in the teacher's lounge was remarkable. Every teacher in the building had immediately noticed him and began commenting on his confidence and charm. They assumed that he was smart and advised his teacher that it might be tough to keep up with him, as well as to keep the other children from gravitating toward him. Of course, they really didn't know much about him yet; all of their impressions were formed from brief glances as he walked into the building or strutted down the hall. Charmers are like that; they get noticed right away and convey an air of ability that may or may not be accurate. Adults talk about them as if they are much older than they really are, often assuming a maturity that is not necessarily there.

Charmers have an amazing way of attracting attention wherever they go: in the classroom, on the stage, or just walking around the mall. People want to give them things and do things for them for no particular reason. They are usually very charming and generally enjoy a great deal of popularity among those around them. Like Magnets, people want to be with them and be like them. But Charmers differ from Magnets in that they don't have a need to lead and control others; they just want to be the center of attention for being themselves. And unlike Magnets, Charmers inspire an awe and a bit of distance because of their luminescence. Those around them tend to idolize them and can feel inferior to them.

See if you are in the midst of a Charmer by answering the following questions.

- ✔ Do heads turn when your child walks by?

- ✔ Do people comment that they just can't take their eyes off of your child when he performs, makes presentations, or is otherwise in the spotlight?

- ✔ Do other children try to imitate your child by dressing like him, getting their hair cut like him, or mimicking his behavior?

- ✔ Is your child able to charm his way out of trouble?

- ✔ Is your child very popular yet lacks close, meaningful relationships with peers?

If you answered "yes" to at least three of these questions, you may be raising a Charmer. Life can be easy for your child if he has brilliance in this area, but you will need to be vigilant in your efforts to require him to develop skills that will enable him to translate his area of brilliance into true accomplishment as he moves through the world.

Warriors

Matt never walked. He began running at age 10 months and never stopped. By the time he was just over a year old, he could throw and catch a ball. As he grew, he continued to amaze everyone with his physical capabilities. He was agile and strong and had incredible hand-eye coordination. He liked to move and had difficulty sitting still at a desk. He learned best when his whole body was involved in a task. He was fearless and enjoyed jumping, leaping, climbing, pushing, pulling—anything that allowed him to push his body to ever-greater limits.

As Matt grew, he wasn't satisfied being involved in just one sport. He wanted to be on every team, and he was usually the star of each one. Coaches sought him out and even tried to manipulate the recreation leagues so they could include him on their rosters. Although Matt enjoyed his star status, it was not really his priority. He just wanted to play, and play hard. It was just as challenging to get him to come inside for dinner as it was to get him off the field if he had an injury—and like most Warriors, he tended to get quite a few injuries. By the time he was a teenager, he had broken several bones, had incurred countless bruises and sprains, and had gotten a concussion. Matt's mother frequently tried to cut back his sporting activities, but as soon as she denied Matt participation on an organized team, he satisfied his need for competition by creating his own challenges, such as turning his neighborhood into an obstacle course for his skateboard. So Matt's mother learned how to mitigate the risks of sports injuries by working with coaches to ensure her son's safety as best she could.

Warriors are typically the kids who really stand out on the sports teams. You can also spot them on any playground. They are the ones who master each piece of equipment before anyone else. They are usually daredevils who cannot be contained or stopped. A Warrior seems fueled by the adrenaline of competition or the inherent danger of a particular activity. Be sure that your Warrior has an opportunity to grow and learn in his activity of choice in as safe a way as possible.

See if you can answer "yes" to at least three of the questions below to determine if you are raising a Warrior.

- ✔ Did your child achieve gross-motor milestones at an early age? Did he walk before 11 months? Ride a tricycle before age three or a bicycle before age four?

- ✔ Does your child seem to be in perpetual motion?

- ✔ Does your child constantly push physical boundaries—running, leaping, jumping, reaching, etc.—in new ways that seem beyond what you thought he could do?

- ✔ Is your child a risk taker? Do you find yourself constantly worried that he will break a bone or a tooth or worse?

- ✔ Do your child's athletic skills seem advanced? Is he able to do things on sports teams a lot better than the other children his age?

These are all characteristics of a Warrior. Get ready—you will not be able to slow down any time soon if you have one of these high-energy kids in your home!

Summing It Up

By reading the descriptions of the different ways in which children can shine, and by taking the quizzes that followed each one, you have probably been able to identify your child's area(s) of brilliance. Read on to see what you can do to spark your child's particular interest(s) in a way that will ensure a happy, productive childhood and future.

CHAPTER 3

Sparks: Igniting Your Child's Passions

You have identified an area of brilliance in your child, and you want to be sure to give her every opportunity to use this gift to its fullest advantage. How can you spark her interests in this area? What can you do to ensure that she develops it into a fulfilling aspect of her life?

First of all, relax. Each decision you make as a parent will not, all by itself, make or break your child. As parents, we worry that we will damage our kids at every turn. The truth is, your child's destiny is shaped by the sum of all of her experiences. With the exception of extremely traumatic events, a single experience will not create or deny success for your child. Second, do not fall into the trap of connecting your child's area of brilliance with a potential career. Focusing on how one makes money is perhaps the best way to snuff out a spark. Very few of us are really motivated by money. Children especially do not respond to comments like, "You will be able to have a great career if you...."

Your goal is to find sparks—those things that make your child's eyes light up and her body dance around like a sparkler on a hot summer night. You want her to be excited about trying things, doing things, and being true to herself. Creating sparks is probably the most fun you can have as a parent. Your brilliant child needs you to constantly be on the lookout for opportunities for her. Everywhere you go, everyone you meet, every newspaper article you read can yield clues of what could be exciting for your child.

Each area of brilliance needs a different type of spark. Some children need organized programs with large groups that are structured into very specialized activities. Others require private lessons or individual experiences to spark their interests. Still others simply need places and situations where they can explore, tinker, and invent. Consider the following:

Things to Do: What are some fun and interesting things to do inside your home and in the community?

Places to Visit: Where will your child want to spend time in your community and beyond? What are some places, familiar and new, where she will feel that she truly belongs?

People to Meet: Who are some other children and adults who share the same area of brilliance as your child? How can you get your child access to people who truly understand her and can encourage her to develop in a positive way?

Structured Activities: What formal lessons or structured activities will be important for your brilliant child? How much of these should you provide? When does a structured activity actually snuff out your child's spark?

Unstructured Time: How can you create an environment that sparks your child's interest and provides the right amount of time for her to explore on her own, in her own way?

This chapter contains ideas that might prompt sparks for the different types of brilliant children.

Storytellers: Nurturing Language Brilliance

Storytellers are inspired by words, and they need to have opportunities to inspire others in this way. They should be encouraged to read as much as possible, write as much as possible, and engage in all kinds of storytelling, like poetry, drama, music, and film. Storytellers require a great deal of time alone to read and create their own stories, as well as a balance of time when they can talk with others and sort through stories and ideas.

Everything these language-loving children see, hear, and do seems to relate to a story. They have vivid imaginations and are always immersed in the stories in their heads. As very young children, many of them act out their stories. You may find them wearing pots as hats and using the cardboard tubes from paper towels as swords. They will play out elaborate and dramatic scenarios with dolls or other toy figures, making them princesses, kings, knights, or unicorns. They will turn a bed into a great sailing ship and a trash can into a throne. These kids cannot stop creating characters and inventing new worlds.

Language is the key to sparking the Storyteller. So whatever you do with her, be sure you give her the chance to talk to you about it. When she tells a story, listen carefully, show interest, and ask questions. Take her to plays and films, and encourage her to write her own. Be sure you spend time at libraries and find interesting subjects online to continue to spark her interests.

Things to Do: These children like anything that involves imagination. Join your child in creating new worlds in the living room or backyard. Look at the clouds, and see if you can create characters out of the moving images. Invent games to play in the car involving rhyming or storytelling. Read books together, and encourage your Storyteller to write her own stories. If she's too young to write, have her dictate to you, and you write the stories for her. Do anything and everything that involves telling real or not-so-real stories.

Places to Visit: Expose your Storyteller to experiences that will appeal to her sense of language. These children enjoy trips to libraries and bookstores so that they can browse the books and choose what they might like to read. You should also take your Storyteller to see movies, plays, puppet shows, and concerts. She may want to ask you questions about what she is seeing, which might disturb others around you, so be sure to talk with her ahead of time and explain that you won't be able to talk while things like plays or movies are taking place. Reserve time afterward to answer all of her questions so that she can process what she has seen.

People to Meet: Take advantage of any opportunity that allows your child to meet authors, playwrights, movie directors, poets, or song writers. If you live in a place where there are few book signings or other events that provide these opportunities, go to author websites. Many adult Storytellers encourage contact from fans. Help your child connect with them online.

Structured Activities: Select activities for your child that will engage her in a way that will not squash her imagination. Look for opportunities in theater and creative problem solving. Groups like Odyssey of the Mind (www.odysseyofthemind.com) are also enticing for these children.

Unstructured Time: Perhaps more than any other group, Storytellers need the constant attention of other people. They need to talk in order to process things. Sharing meals and just spending unstructured time together with a Storyteller is vital to her development. If you don't happen to share the interests of your child in this category, find someone who does so that she will be able to process what she is thinking with someone else. When your Storyteller wants to tell you a story, or have you tell her a story, be sure to take the time to do so.

A Storyteller is constantly experiencing an alternate reality to yours. She is usually lost in an imaginary world of her own making and will need time alone to think, read, and write about it. She may benefit from a less rigid and controlled home environment, where she is free to be herself and create the characters that gnaw at her to be born. Be sure that your daily schedule includes time without programmed activities and that you provide at least one day a week when your Storyteller is not required to be part of an organized group. These children need to get lost in books and in their own thoughts in order to truly develop their storytelling brilliance.

Selecting appropriate reading material, movies, plays, and music for a Storyteller to experience is the key to success. She will want to follow her interests, which will likely be more mature than her same-age peers. This can be a rather tricky issue. As the parent of a Storyteller, you need to keep an open mind about the content of books, movies, and other media so that your child can experience what she needs to keep up with her own storytelling abilities. Keep checking yourself on these decisions. If exposure to certain material results in a change in behavior, fears, or extreme emotions, the content is not appropriate. As your child tries new things, keep a close watch on the impact they have on her, and adjust accordingly.

Calculators: Nurturing Mathematical Brilliance

Calculators are constantly trying to make sense of the world. They enjoy logic and organization, and they need opportunities to solve problems and exercise their natural tendency to organize things. From a very young age, they crave experiences that allow them to sort and put things together. Encourage your young

Calculator to explore all of the ways that math and logic can be used to solve problems.

Things to Do: Calculators need you to provide them with lots of puzzles and games that allow them to exercise their need to solve problems. They enjoy anything that requires logic and are fascinated with fitting things together. As they grow older, you can continue to challenge them with computer games that involve logic, Sudoku puzzles, or other numerical games. Enlist their help in organizing things in the house or solving budgeting dilemmas. Your Calculator likes to put order into the world. Provide him with opportunities to do so.

Places to Visit: With their organized brains, Calculators like anything that emphasizes order and logic. Any place that is an engineering or architectural marvel will be especially interesting to this group. They enjoy visiting places like the Horseshoe Curve in Altoona, Pennsylvania (where trains careen around a mountain on a track in the shape of a horseshoe), or watching the workings of the locks of a canal. Other potential destinations include Hoover Dam, the Empire State Building, and the recently constructed bridge across the Colorado River connecting Arizona and Nevada. Any museum that displays equipment with functionality, such as armor, weapons, vehicles, or tools, might also be of interest to the Calculator. A word of caution: Do not force these kids to read everything in the museum. Let them wander and enjoy without feeling compelled to tell them about everything. They do not particularly enjoy stories.

People to Meet: Calculators tend not to be highly social. If your child prefers being alone much of the time and does not seem anxious when relating with others, there is no need to worry. You may just want to occasionally assist him in making connections with others so that he develops the social skills necessary to get along in the world. Calculators tend to gravitate toward their math and science teachers, and they also usually enjoy music. Help your Calculator make connections by capitalizing on opportunities to play in musical groups or join activities led by favorite teachers. On the other hand, if socializing causes great stress and your child suffers whenever he is forced to engage with peers, there may be something more going on. An online resource that can be quite helpful in this situation is www.sengifted.org. If the problem seems serious, it may be appropriate to discuss the situation with counselors or other professionals.

Structured Activities: Many Calculators love music, so provide lessons and access to musical groups at school and in the community. They also tend to like robotics and quirky games that have become popular in recent years, like cup stacking, and they are usually good at games involving logic, such as chess. See what clubs involving these types of games are available in your community. If there aren't any, consider starting one so that your Calculator will have access to activities that are engaging and meaningful for him.

Unstructured Time: Calculators can struggle with unstructured time and usually don't need or want much of it. Be sure to have plenty of things around the house that will engage your child in logic and organization, including puzzles and games like chess and Sudoku. Provide access to lots of music, and be sure your Calculator has an instrument to play just for fun without a lot of pressure to practice. And don't be stingy purchasing apps for your mobile device. However, although these children can benefit greatly from spending their time working on puzzles or number games, be sure that these activities don't consume them and become their only way to occupy time; they need to go outdoors and play once in a while too!

Explorers: Nurturing Scientific Brilliance

Explorers are a fun group. They tend to be the geeky kids on the block who want to know how everything works. They can be exhausting to parents because they are always asking "why" and need lots of time and attention in their quest to learn everything, right now, while you are cooking dinner or replying to emails from your boss. Explorers need lots of opportunities to think deeply about things and solve problems. Be sure to provide your young Explorer with the time and space to do this on his own, and also some formal structures where he can problem-solve with other Explorers. Provide your Explorer with access to the Internet and visits to places that will ignite his curiosity, and follow his lead to discover and make connections.

> *Things to Do:* Explorers often enjoy cooking because it involves experimentation within a set of guidelines. Teach them basic principles, and then let them figure things out for themselves. They also like to build things and put things together in interesting ways. Robotics, computer programming, sound engineering, and microscopes are just a few of the many subjects of interest to most Explorers.

> *Places to Visit:* Anywhere and everywhere is interesting to Explorers, but they usually don't engage in the way one might expect. For example, if you go to an art museum, an Explorer might be fascinated by the mechanics of the lights used in an exhibit but have absolutely no interest at all in the actual art. These children are very inexpensive to entertain. They are thrilled to walk under a bridge and see how it supports the weight on top of it. They marvel at watching ants at work or seeing construction workers in action. Take them anywhere anytime, and follow their lead to see what is interesting to them. They usually enjoy technology stores, medical supply stores, and other places containing gadgets. If they have an interest in boats, you might want to spend time at a marine supply store; if they

like cars, an auto parts store. They like to know what makes things work and enjoy any place where they can explore.

People to Meet: Any geek will do. Consider your Explorer's specific interests. If he likes cars, introduce him to the best mechanics in town. If he enjoys cooking, find a chef who wouldn't mind talking with a young person. If he is a CSI nut, think about introducing him to a medical examiner.

Structured Activities: Explorers tend to enjoy structured activities where they can be in charge of the things they experience. Scouts are a good idea for these children because they can pick badges of interest and pursue the activities in a way that is right for them. They also enjoy competitions involving problem solving, and many organizations and programs for students focus on this type of thing, including Future Problem Solving (www.fpspi.org), Odyssey of the Mind (www.odysseyofthemind.com), and specialty camps for children with interests in science.

Unstructured Time: Make sure your Explorer has plenty of time alone to explore. Take your cues from his interests, provide the raw materials, and then get out of the way. For example, if he enjoys building things, give him Legos and tinker toys. If he enjoys scientific exploration, give him a microscope and other related tools so that he can conduct his own inquiries and experiments. These children have great difficulty stopping the creative process and don't want to put things away, so provide some space with shelving or boards that can be slid into a corner to allow him to continue his projects over time.

Magnets: Nurturing Leadership Brilliance

Magnets will naturally find a group of followers. No matter where they are, they will end up telling others what to do and creating a social strata. Sometimes they seem to be—or actually are—bossy. You need to make sure that your Magnet can express her leadership abilities in ways that are healthy and that attract others, not repel them. Help her become part of organizations that value input and leadership from young members so that she has opportunities to lead and inspire. Teach her what she can do with this incredible gift and how it can be used across a variety of fields. A Magnet should be encouraged to develop her skills so that she will be prepared for the inevitable opportunities that will present themselves. Help her explore a wide range of subjects that can ignite her passions and give her a sense of purpose.

> *Things to Do:* You won't have to direct a Magnet very much; she will likely try to direct you. Just follow her lead, which will typically involve organizing others in some sort of fun activity, and help her adjust to meet the needs of others in the group. Allow her to experience natural consequences from her mistakes, so long as the mistakes will not cause danger to all involved. For example, if she is taking the lead on planning a camping trip and forgets things that might make the trip more enjoyable, such as games or instruments, it will still be fine. Everyone will just have to figure out what to do for fun. On the other hand, you would need to step in if she forgets personal flotation devices on a canoeing trip. The rule of thumb is that if a decision will result in minor discomfort or difficulty, let your Magnet learn from her mistakes. Anything that causes a risk to life and limb requires adult intervention!

> *Places to Visit:* Magnets can find pleasure in visiting any type of museum, attraction, or even retail stores. The key to engaging a Magnet is to let her be in charge. Talk about where you are going ahead of time, and ask her to set the agenda and lead you and anyone else in your group in the activities of the day. Use this as an opportunity to teach your Magnet to think about the needs of others in the group and to ensure that everyone has a voice.

People to Meet: Help your young Magnet meet adult Magnets. Think of leaders in your community. These might be politicians, business owners, or professionals. Talk about what these people have done to use their magnetism for the good of the community. It will be good for your Magnet to become a student of human behavior and to learn how she can become influential to make the world a better place. Consider helping your Magnet take part in volunteer organizations that really make a difference, such as Habitat for Humanity or the American Red Cross. Let her see adult Magnets at work!

Structured Activities: A Magnet is sparked by being part of a large group. Your Magnet will want to be part of organized activities that have very social aspects to them and where she can be around lots of other children. Seek opportunities for her to be involved in teams and groups where she will naturally assume a leadership role. Sports teams, theatrical productions, student government, scouts, and other activities can all provide these types of experiences.

Unstructured Time: You will also want to provide time and space for your Magnet to have informal groups of friends. This can easily happen in a neighborhood where groups of children get together in a park, cul-de-sac, or playground. Some parents may be tempted to keep their child safe by not letting her play outside with groups of kids without strict adult oversight, but this kind of "safety" will keep your young Magnet from being able to really experience the leadership that will spark her to develop her amazing quality. If you live in a place where children can't really congregate or play in public spaces, then make your home the place where kids will want to come. Just giving your Magnet a space where all of her friends can mingle will provide her with opportunities to develop her leadership.

Just be sure that everyone in the house gets time for what is important for them.

Designers: Nurturing Artistic Brilliance

Designers are artists who view the world with an eye for beauty or expression. You will want to create an environment where your Designer can express herself visually and drink in the visual stimulation around her. She should have some artistic materials to use—items like butcher paper, tempera paints, an easel for young children, and more extensive media to experiment with as she grows and continues to explore. Most Designers enjoy making things like puppets, paintings, beaded jewelry, collages, textiles, or items crafted of recycled materials.

Your Designer needs you to assist her in continually exploring her creative side. Help her access instruction, mentors, and experiences that will propel her forward in her medium of choice. Create a world that has a healthy balance of academic and artistic experiences so that she can become a well-balanced adult.

Things to Do: Take your Designer to plays or musicals to enjoy visually interesting costumes and stage sets. Visit botanical gardens, parks, or sculpture gardens with aesthetically appealing features. Seek out movies on the big screen that are visually stimulating. If you don't already have one, consider getting a high-definition television for your home that will allow meaningful home-theater experiences. Although it is counter-intuitive, Designers do not always enjoy formal art lessons. This is true particularly when they are young. Think of art as something that has to be experienced rather than taught, especially when your Designer is young. Instead of lessons, encourage your Designer to create at every opportunity.

Places to Visit: Designers enjoy any place that has lots of visual stimulation. They usually love visiting places that have natural beauty, as well as art museums—as long as you follow their lead and allow them to explore by seeing and not by reading or being talked at. They also tend to enjoy aquariums where they can watch fish moving across large panes of glass. Sometimes they like mundane places like shopping malls, as long as they are aesthetically pleasing. When you experience these things, be sure to allow your Designer plenty of time to take it all in. She may not verbally express what she is seeing, but she truly is absorbing it all. Designers also like visiting places that look very different from their own community. If you live in the country, take your Designer to the city. In general, it is good for your Designer to see lots of different places that will appeal to her visually.

People to Meet: Designers can often be viewed as a little bit eccentric. They need to be around people with good senses of humor who will be completely accepting of who they are. People who are interested in your Designer's art and who enjoy being with unusual people will be good for your young Designer.

Structured Activities: Your Designer will likely not need much in the way of structured activities, particularly when she is younger. As she grows, you will want to find activities for her that encourage creativity and self-expression. These might be designing sets or costumes for the school play, creating a community mural, or putting together a holiday display for a local charity. Once your Designer reaches high school, you will want to ensure that she has competent instruction from an artist who will assist her in pursuing her medium of choice.

Unstructured Time: Like Storytellers, Designers need lots of time alone so that they can create, and you will likely find that your Designer needs more alone time than most other children. Her imagination is constantly at work, but unlike Storytellers, she usually does not have the need to put everything into words; she is pensive and expressive in other ways. She may spend hours just staring at something. You may believe that she's wasting time, but she is not. She is taking in every detail of an object, thinking about its color, form, and texture. She is planning what she will create next and how she will create it. To do this, she needs to interact with objects and use all of her senses to take in the information. So just like for Storytellers, it is critical for her to have large blocks of alone time each day, and perhaps a full day each week, to allow for this.

Your Designer needs to have appropriate materials to express herself. But don't worry; you need not purchase expensive art supplies. A Designer's best friend is often the drawing pad. When she is very young, just be sure to always have plenty of different kinds of art supplies available, like crayons, colored pencils, markers, and paints. The cheap stuff from discount stores is fine at this point. Perhaps you can paint a wall in her room with blackboard paint that allows her to use chalk. Start a recycling bin in your home so that you can collect things that might be intriguing and useful for art projects—paper, string, wrapping paper, bits of cloth and ribbon, rubber bands, twisties—anything that she might use to create. This bin will become a continual source of inspiration for her because she will never know what she is going to find in it.

Provide space in your home to allow your Designer's self-expression. You will also want to create a place in your Designer's room to store her creations as she is working on them. These children have difficulty staying organized and keeping their works-in-progress out of harm's way— particularly if they have siblings. So if space allows, set up a large table or shelves where projects can "live" as she works on them.

Melody Makers: Nurturing Musical Brilliance

Your home will never be quiet if a Melody Maker lives there. These children hear music in everything and are constantly creating it. Be sure that your Melody Maker always has access to musical experiences, musical instruction, musical mentors, and musical friends. Music for this group is not an "extra"; it is truly their life's blood.

The key to sparking a Melody Maker is exposure to lots and lots of different types of music and different types of instruments. They need to know what is out there—way beyond the pop tunes on the radio. Provide your Melody Maker with experiences that involve a wide variety of styles of music and instruments, ensuring that he will learn to discern what is higher quality for each genre. You will want to take him to concerts where he can see and hear professionals perform and can learn to develop an ear for good music. As your child becomes more interested, provide opportunities for him to learn to read music. This will help him experience it in as many ways as possible.

> *Things to Do:* Browse through YouTube to see all sorts of music performances: opera, choirs, orchestras, bands of all kinds—classical, pop, rock, reggae, and more. Explore music of different countries, like Africa, Cuba, and Mexico. Play different kinds of music while in the car. Make instruments from found objects, and be sure to have things in your home that let your Melody Maker create music. Inexpensive keyboards are a favorite of this group of children, especially if they also create sounds that simulate other instruments besides just a piano. Do fun experiments with sound or rhythm. Create a band of water glasses by filling each one to a different level and hitting it with a spoon to make a sound. Old empty boxes make great percussion instruments.

> *Places to Visit:* You will want to take your Melody Maker to concerts of all kinds, festivals or other gatherings of

musicians, and musical theater productions. Movies with especially good soundtracks will be appealing, too.

People to Meet: Find out who the musicians are in your community. There are teachers in just about every school system who also play in bands. There are also musical groups of all ages and in every town. Expose your child to others who share the same passion.

Structured Activities: Does your child's school have a music program? Be sure you know what is available there first. If there is no program, consider working with school leaders to create one using volunteers and small grants from local businesses. You would be amazed at how many people are willing to give to this type of cause. For the long-term, get active in your school's parent organizations, and demand with other parents that music become part of the curriculum for all children.

Outside of school, private lessons are always a good idea to help develop the talents of Melody Makers. Find the best teachers available in your community, and do what you can to get at least one lesson a week for your child. You can also look for community orchestras or choirs, which typically require an audition before participating. Many religious institutions have choirs or orchestras available for interested members to join. Consider any musical groups, camps, or activities at school that will keep your Melody Maker moving in the right direction.

Unstructured Time: Melody Makers need plenty of unstructured time to experiment with sound. Although formal practice and lessons are important, so is just having fun. In fact, most Melody Makers gain more from just messing around with instruments and singing than they do with formal activities. At the age of four, our daughter started each day singing along to her favorite musical theater songs. She imagined that she was a character in each show and sang and danced around the room as she got ready for school. This type of unbridled fun has the potential to produce the skills that your growing Melody Maker needs, so be sure you allow this to happen. Many kids who never "practice" but spend tons of time immersed in music that just feels good can ultimately become great musicians.

Butterflies: Nurturing Dance Brilliance

You can't miss the Butterflies. These children never walk anywhere. They flit and flutter, skip, jump, and hop their way through the world. They are constantly moving and experience the world by feeling it with their whole bodies. Whenever music begins to play, they instinctively begin swaying and tapping their feet. The key to raising a Butterfly is helping her to keep moving. Butterflies also tend to enjoy gymnastics, ice skating, and roller skating. Anything that involves the whole body in choreographed movements is a spark for a Butterfly.

Be sure that you don't neglect your little boy Butterfly. There is an assumption that a boy on the move will be an athlete, which may be true. But there are lots of boys who are Butterflies, not Warriors, and they need to be encouraged the same way we encourage our girls. *Any* child can be a Warrior *or* a Butterfly. It is by no means gender specific. Be sure you identify your child's area of brilliance correctly and develop it well, even if it is inconsistent with gender (or other) stereotypes that might be present in the community.

> *Things to Do:* You will want to take your Butterfly to see dance productions. It is difficult for very young children to really understand the point of what they are doing unless they have an opportunity to see grown-up dancers in action. I once sat with a little Butterfly during a professional ballet production. She had taken ballet for about a year but had never seen real dancers perform. Suddenly she turned to her mother and said, "Oh…*that's* ballet!"

Every community has dance schools that do annual recitals. Many places offer *The Nutcracker* during the holidays. Be sure your Butterfly gets to see experienced dancers in action!

Places to Visit: These children love to go to parks where they can tiptoe on the edges of play equipment and retaining walls, fly over small bridges, and interact with physical objects. You will want to find the playgrounds (indoor or outdoor) that have the most interesting obstacles and fun things that allow children's bodies to move in different ways. You should also take your Butterfly to movies that highlight dance to get her even more interested in how to use her body. There are plenty of wonderful dance movies available for adolescents and even younger children, such as *Fame* and *High School Musical*. The term "Butterfly" here is about how the child uses her body; a Butterfly may or may not be a "social butterfly" in the way that phrase is used. The key to raising a Butterfly is to get her out of the house and moving as much as possible so she can experience the world in the best way for her.

People to Meet: Similar to Melody Makers, these children need to be around other Butterflies. Find dance groups in your community or playgroups with an emphasis on physical activities. See if your school has any groups that focus on dance. If it doesn't have such a group, consider starting one.

Structured Activities: Dance lessons are a must for the Butterfly. They will help her develop her skills and learn new types of dance. Be sure she gets exposure to lots of different types of dance, including ballet, jazz, tap, hip hop, etc. She will eventually settle on a favorite. Many communities offer dance classes through recreation departments or after-school programs. Find one that focuses on fun and exploration when she is just beginning. As she grows, you will want to investigate more professional types of programs. It is critical that you find a dance studio where your child can learn from someone who really understands dance. Many studios focus more on the end-of-year recital with tacky costumes (where they make a great deal of income) than on the actual dance instruction. While there is certainly nothing inherently wrong with being in a recital, you want to be sure your Butterfly is getting good instruction with appropriate feedback along the way. You want a dance instructor who will correct her over and over until she gets it right. The instructor should be tough and demand excellence. In our "soft" culture, you may hear young dancers complain that an instructor is mean and yells at them. Of course you don't want someone who is really nasty or who ridicules young children, but the dance instructor *should* bark orders, telling your child when she is not doing things right and demanding perfection. This is the only way a good dancer will become great.

Some professional programs are expensive, but if your Butterfly really is talented, it's important to try to work something out so that she has access to these higher-level experiences. If your Butterfly is a boy, ask for a scholarship. Since there is always a shortage of males in class, scholarships are often provided for talented boys. Because many productions depend on a certain number of male dancers, schools are always anxious to recruit them by offering financial incentives.

If a Butterfly is of the caliber to become a principal in a professional ballet company, it is sometimes wise to enter the company at a very young age, skipping college and sometimes even the end of high school. If this is the best path for your young Butterfly, be sure that she continues her education through online courses or other educational options, allowing her to develop her mind as well as her body.

Unstructured Time: Most Butterflies want to be with other Butterflies a great deal and need to find a studio or class to call home. They may want to just hang around this place, even during times when they don't have lessons scheduled. This is a good thing. It allows connection and camaraderie with peers. It lets the Butterfly watch and learn from other dancers. But most importantly, it provides her with a safe place where she truly belongs. Encourage your Butterfly to be in this environment as much as possible. At home, be sure to allow time and space for her to spread her wings. If your home has a basement or garage, consider turning it into a small dance studio. All it takes is a little flooring (laminate with a good cushion underneath will do) that you can install yourself, a couple of mirrors on the wall, and a ballet bar made from a dowel. Just having this space to call her own will do wonders for a Butterfly. If you don't have a home where this is possible, consider just putting up a bar and mirror in her bedroom so she can stretch and imagine.

Charmers: Nurturing Performance Brilliance

Charmers are those who seem to draw the world's attention to them. They are the ones who are "loved" by the camera, who are both photogenic and videogenic. When they are on stage, the audience members can't take their eyes off them. When they walk into a room, everyone turns to see them. They are the kids who literally can take your breath away by their presence. They are different from Magnets because they have an inapproachable quality to them and attract those who would idolize them rather than follow them. You want to ensure that you are constantly on the lookout for people who might exploit them or do them harm.

Your Charmer needs a life that allows her to be in the spotlight and to use her abilities for good. Be sure she understands that being a Charmer brings with it some unwanted attention, as well as a huge responsibility to do good things. Encourage her to pursue a wide array of studies and experiences so that she can move toward things that will bring purpose to her life. Require her to develop her skills in communicating, collaborating, and problem solving so that she will be positioned well to take advantage of the many opportunities that will certainly present themselves as she grows up.

Things to Do: Keeping your Charmer grounded while also encouraging her aspirations is a difficult balancing act. You should have lots of conversations about values and character and the kind of person she is on the inside. If your Charmer tends to idolize other Charmers who are famous, be sure to talk about the real human characteristics of these individuals. There is always someone famous in the news who is talented in acting or performing but who has made some bad choices; use these tabloid stories as cautionary tales. What could have prevented these problems? What are some of the difficulties that come with fame? At the same time, you might want to pretend to have premiers and fashion shows at your house. Recruit some friends, and really have fun with it! Let your Charmer visualize and act out the big life she really wants.

Places to Visit: Charmers are attracted to things that we usually connect with fame and fortune. They like to see incredible places and experience high-end living. They enjoy being in cosmopolitan areas where they can experience designer stores and expensive restaurants. Don't worry if you are not wealthy yourself. You can still give your Charmer a taste of these experiences, and you should. Those of us who are not wealthy sometimes get caught up in a mindset that wealth is bad and should be discouraged, but Charmers are drawn to this world, and they need to see and experience it. It is your job as a parent to help them understand that money is not good or bad; it is how one uses it that is important. So take your Charmer to the nearest town with designer stores and talk with her about what you experience together. If you can't afford dinner at a fancy restaurant, go and have dessert there. Use these types of experiences as a springboard for conversations about values and character. Remember, money isn't a bad thing, but a Charmer wants that exciting world that she believes comes with it. Be sure to help her understand what money can and can't do, as well as how it can change people for the worse if they allow that to happen.

People to Meet: You will want your Charmer to be exposed to people who are living the life that she aspires to. Think about people you know who are close to this. This might be tricky if you are living in a typical suburb or rural community. However, you might be surprised. Every town usually has someone in it who had another more exotic life before settling into a quiet little burg. Think about everyone you know, and see if your child might be able to connect with someone nearby who has experienced some of these things. If not, don't give up. There are always opportunities to hear speakers or attend events where Charmers are available to meet the public. As you meet other Charmers, help your child see their true qualities, both the good and the not-so-good, that make them "real" people. You want to raise your Charmer to be a happy, healthy, well-balanced adult, not a narcissist or someone that you have to work to manage.

Structured Activities: Charmers are usually drawn to acting and modeling. There are lots of opportunities for acting in most communities. Get your Charmer involved with community theater or school theater. Take advantage of summer camps or after-school clubs with this focus. Many department stores recruit local children to participate in modeling events to show off their seasonal collections, and these can be excellent opportunities for your Charmer to try modeling. Beware of pageants and competitions. You may end up spending tons of money for experiences that could be damaging to your Charmer. Unfortunately, there are some acting, modeling, and pageant groups that encourage or accept nasty, cut-throat behavior that may be a negative influence on your child. With each activity, consider how it will contribute to the development of your child's character. You want your Charmer to always understand that she must be kind to others and support their successes.

Unstructured Time: Give your Charmer access to media creation. Charmers love to experiment with pictures and video and create images of themselves. Encourage your Charmer to think about how others see her, and help her to develop meaningful relationships. Talk about things that good friends do, and work with her to create friendships based on what she has in common with others and what she can give of herself. Allow your home to be the place where other kids gather so your Charmer can develop the social connections so important to children who tend to inspire idolization.

Warriors: Nurturing Athletic Brilliance

Ah, the Warrior—that fearless kid who jumps and runs and moves assertively without apology through the world. This child is strong and agile and fast. To her, everything becomes a physical challenge to be overcome. Warriors needs lots of wide open space and opportunities to explore. They also need coaches and parents who stress a love of the game and the values it instills above anything else. A Warrior's preparation in sports should be balanced with academic learning.

Warriors need to be around other Warriors who will push them to become even better every step of the way. It is tempting when a Warrior is very young to engage in high competition a little too early, but be careful about involving her in more than one sports league at a time, and about pushing her to fulfill *your* dreams. If she tires of a particular sport, try another one, and don't discount the less traditional sports that may not be quite as popular in your community. The key to raising a Warrior is to provide lots of opportunities for her to move and challenge herself, while also having fun and developing solid values—on the field and off.

Things to Do: Most Warriors will find a sport or two early in life that really sparks them. Give your Warrior a wide variety of athletic experiences so she can see what is most exciting for her. These can be traditional sports teams or more individual sports like tennis, wrestling, ice skating, surfing, or snowboarding.

Places to Visit: Take your Warrior anywhere she can move and experience the world with her whole body. Find places where there are enough barriers so that you can supervise her, yet let her run independently.

People to Meet: Your Warrior needs to be around other Warrior children and adults who will be rough and tumble with her yet will not injure her. She also needs to be able to meet athletes who can guide her. These can be golf pros, swimming coaches, or simply people who participate in triathlons or other sports. Every community has a few athletes who will understand your Warrior. Get her access to these people.

Structured Activities: Be careful with just how much your Warrior participates in organized teams and how much you push. Many parents of Warriors make a huge mistake in this area. They enroll their child in every competitive team in the chosen sport until the child finally has had enough. Remember, you want to spark her interest, not snuff it out. Just one team per season is plenty at the level of competition that your child really enjoys.

Unstructured Time: This is pretty easy for Warriors. Your job is to get out of the way. Although most parents tend to want to protect their children, the parent of a Warrior really has to fight that urge. Your child is different. She can handle a little more risk than others. Oh, and by the way, she will get hurt. That just goes with the territory. So think of yourself as an insurance underwriter. How much and what types of risk are you willing to let your Warrior have? Think of the non-negotiable items that must always be in place, like helmets for biking, skateboarding, and snowboarding. Think about the locations of the activities and how much risk you can mitigate. Think about who can supervise these activities to reduce the risk—and then you have to let go. Let your Warrior do what she needs to do to experience the world.

Lighting the Spark

Your job as a parent of a brilliant child is to provide access to people, places, and things that will spark his interests. You need to encourage without pushing, guide without leading, and give your child the time and space to experiment and explore in the best way for him. This is the most fun anyone can possibly have as a parent, so savor every moment!

Don't confuse sparks with formal education. Although you may have your child enrolled in formal activities, many of the ideas I've described as sparks take place outside of the traditional school environment. School can spark your child, but it often snuffs out the spark, too, by putting time limits or other restrictions on projects or activities, or by providing too few hands-on or creative learning opportunities. Read on to learn how you can work together with school personnel to ensure that your child's education will help to nurture brilliance.

Chapter 4

Diamond Cutting: Education that Brings Out and Polishes Brilliance

A diamond starts out as a rough stone. It takes a skilled diamond cutter using precision tools, special training, expertise, and hard work to turn it into a sparkling gem. A brilliant child needs to have an education much like diamond cutting—one that will bring out and polish facets that capture the child's light to create a sparkling gem. It is the parent's responsibility to monitor the education process with vigilance, ensuring that the child is developing in a way that will capture her brilliance and allow it to shine.

Demarcus just couldn't sit still. As soon as he entered the classroom each day, he darted around like a pinball, responding to each light, sound, and touch. When the teacher introduced something new, his eyes lit up and his mouth became a Gatling gun, peppering the teacher with question after question after question. The other children just stared at him; he was the strangest kid they had ever seen. He made weird noises and moved in an awkward way. And those questions. Couldn't he just shut up? What in the world made him move and act and talk like that?

What made Demarcus do all of those things was his intensity, his passion, and his insatiable need to learn. His brain needed to be fed with as much sensory information as possible, or he felt like it was starving. The teacher and the other students in his class simply could not keep up with it. Although a school psychologist had determined that Demarcus had an IQ above 140, the teacher did not recommend him for the gifted program. She told Demarcus's mother that the boy needed to get his behavior under control before he could take part in the gifted class. She believed that only children who were "serious" about their learning and who could focus would benefit from the increased rigor that the class demanded. She, and the rest of the child study team, recommended that Demarcus be taken to a pediatrician for evaluation for a possible attention problem.

Demarcus's mother was embarrassed about her child's behavior, and she understood the teacher's and administrators' reluctance to include him in the gifted class. She certainly did not want her son to be responsible for disrupting those other well-behaved children. So she complied and took Demarcus to the doctor.

Demarcus's doctor immediately diagnosed him as having attention deficit hyperactivity disorder, also known as ADHD, and quickly prescribed powerful drugs to help him control his impulses. Demarcus took the medicine, and school became a little easier. He stopped making the weird sounds, and he was able to sit still and focus more on the things his teacher wanted him to do. He asked fewer questions and didn't feel quite as intense as he had before. Although this was somewhat of a relief, he didn't really like it. He complained of feeling "numb" and just not himself. Before the medication, school had held some excitement for Demarcus, but now it was simply something he had to endure.

Since things seemed to have leveled out for her son, Demarcus's mother chose not to pursue placement for him in the gifted program. She feared that the increased rigor of the gifted class might make his behavior worse again, and her goal was to stop getting negative phone calls from the school. Consequently, Demarcus never did participate in gifted classes in elementary school.

Although some children truly suffer from attention disorders and greatly benefit from medication to treat them, Demarcus was not one of them. He was not suffering at all. He had an incredible curiosity about the world and loved learning about it. But when he took the medication, it had its desired effect; he was anesthetized. What Demarcus needed was an appropriate education, not medication.

A good education should be inspiring. Students should be encouraged to think, create, and explore in ways that honor their strengths and passions. Brilliant children like Demarcus benefit from a school where their gifts are recognized and their energy directed. Instead, what Demarcus experienced was a place where adults simply managed his behavior and provided him with classes that he needed to sit still for and endure.

Have you ever watched an exceptional musician when she is playing? She gets into a kind of "zone" that seems to fuel her talent. You can see the same thing with all kinds of artists, athletes, scientists, or anyone who creates or discovers. Some call this intense focus a state of flow. [14] You have probably felt it when you do the things that you love the most. It is that feeling when you are most alive, when you have mastery in a particular area and you just go with it. You become so engrossed in your endeavor that you lose track of time. You may forget to eat meals or sleep at usual times. It is an amazing feeling, and one that is necessary for brilliance to be productive. Demarcus's behavior wasn't misbehavior at all; it was just a young boy with great intensity trying to get into his zone.

Schools that do a good job of creating flow in their students establish environments that are aesthetic. One of Webster's definitions of the word *aesthetic* is "responsive to or appreciative of what is pleasurable to the senses." When something is aesthetic, we learn more because our senses are awakened and ready to receive and interpret information. The more aesthetic and pleasing a learning environment is, the more we will learn. This is why children tend to remember things when we put them into a song or chant or rhyme, or when we play classical music while they write. It pleases their senses. School should be aesthetic, not anesthetic. The key to creating just the right educational experiences for your child is to find a way to make these experiences as aesthetic as possible, capitalizing on your child's natural intensity.

In thinking about the educational needs of brilliant children, it is important to understand student motivation. Most brilliant children who either drop out or disengage to the point of not learning do so because school is no longer relevant to them. They simply are not motivated to learn what is being taught in their classes.[15] They usually are, however, motivated in other areas. They may spend countless hours and great energy exploring their own scientific experiments or reading their favorite authors or working out the tune of a song, but they lack interest in typical schoolwork.

According to Daniel Pink, author of *Drive: The Surprising Truth about What Motivates Us*,[16] motivation for complex cognitive tasks is made up of three factors: autonomy, mastery, and purpose. This is particularly important for brilliant children, whose intensity seems to magnify these concepts. First, these children need the greatest degree of autonomy possible in their area(s) of brilliance. They must feel that they are at least partially in charge of what, when, and where they want to learn. Secondly, their "rage to master"[17] needs to be embraced. The Storyteller who wants to finish writing a play in his English class may feel disrespected and even violated if he is suddenly told to stop so that he can go to his gym class. Finally, many brilliant children need a sense of purpose in order to do their schoolwork. If they don't see a reason to understand or learn something, they simply don't want to waste their time with it. So the challenge is to look at each area of brilliance and see what we can do to make the child's educational experience the best it can be to nurture that brilliance.

Educational Options

It is helpful if you live in an area where some educational options are available. Your first step in identifying the best education for your child is to learn what options already exist. How much choice do you have? Then consider which choice is best for your child. School choice can take many forms. Here are some of the most common:

School programs: Are there specific programs in your zoned public school or school district that might be available for your brilliant child? Acceleration? Enrichment? A pull-out or send-out daily or weekly gifted program? Art, drama, music, or sports programs? Computer classes? Chess? Future Problem Solving? Odyssey of the Mind? Weekend Super Saturdays?

Acceleration: This is perhaps the most unused option, yet it is also probably the most cost-effective one—and one that seems to work the best for most brilliant children. All it takes is flexibility on the part of the school. Let children move ahead to a level that is most appropriate for their area of brilliance. Allow the Designer to participate in art classes with older students, the Storyteller to take part in more advanced English classes, the math whiz to move up a grade or more for math class, and so on. Your middle schooler may be ready for certain high school classes, like algebra or economics, or your high schooler may want to take some college courses through dual enrollment or Advanced Placement options.

Choosing a particular public school: Do you have the right to choose which school your child attends in your district? Does your district have open enrollment? For example, if there is more than one elementary school, do you have the right to choose the one you like? If your neighborhood school has been identified as being in need of improvement due to low standardized test scores, you may be able to choose another school, even if your district doesn't have a formalized school choice program.

Choosing a different public school district: Some states allow families to cross district lines and attend a school in a neighboring or even cross-town district. Check out the rules in your state to learn more, or inquire at neighboring districts to see if they accept students from your district.

Magnet schools: These are schools that are established for the purpose of providing a specialized program like science or fine arts or humanities. Magnet schools came into play as an alternative to forced bussing during years when schools were trying to desegregate. The idea was that a special science program or arts emphasis would attract suburban, non-minority students to inner-city schools with high percentages of minorities, thus helping the school reflect better racial balance. Students from a large geographic area are eligible to attend a magnet school. Find out if any exist in your area, what their special offerings are, and how a child can be enrolled.

Charter schools: A charter school is a public school that can be exempt from certain rules and policies. These schools must have open enrollment for all students and will enroll students by lottery if enrollment exceeds capacity. Charter schools vary widely in their educational philosophies and approaches, so you will want to make sure you understand each specific school to learn if it is appropriate for your brilliant child.

Private schools: These schools are non-public options. They charge tuition since they are not funded publicly, and they have an enrollment process to determine if they are a good fit for each individual student. Many private schools have scholarship programs for low-income students and/or students with disabilities. Private school staff usually love to enroll brilliant children and may have some funds available to award scholarships. Additionally, there are some states and school districts that have voucher programs available for students who meet certain criteria. If you think a private school would be best for your child, be sure to go and talk to the admissions team to learn how it might be affordable for your family. Remember, though, that private does not always mean better, so investigate each school thoroughly before making any decisions.

Homeschooling: This is sometimes the only viable option for brilliant children, particularly for those who are functioning several grade levels ahead of their peers. You may be able to find a home-school cooperative in your community, or you might even start your own to best meet the needs of your child and your family. With the rising popularity of homeschooling, there are now more resources than ever for curriculum, guidance in developing cooperative groups, and understanding how your decisions will affect your child.[18]

Online resources: We now have many ways to harness technology for educational purposes. Most states allow high school students to take some courses online. This is a wonderful option that can be used for acceleration for your brilliant child. Students who utilize this option take a set number of courses in each subject area and can graduate in less than the normal four years. Some states may even allow this option for younger students not yet enrolled in high school. These children can "bank" the credits and apply them once they are chronologically ready for high school. This kind of accelerated learning can really motivate brilliant children. There are also many online resources for younger students. These include formal classes or remediation opportunities, or even full elementary programs for homeschoolers.

Working with Educators

Most teachers want their children to have stimulating experiences in their classrooms that help them to learn and grow intellectually. When this doesn't happen for a particular child, some teachers are simply at a loss as to how to rectify the situation. Sometimes the teacher isn't even aware that the child is bored or lacks interest, especially if the child is compliant and maintains good grades. But parents know when their children are struggling, whether academically or emotionally with a classroom that just doesn't fit with their level of ability. Often, just bringing this information to the attention of teachers is all that is necessary for positive change to happen.

Sometimes, though, teachers can't do what they need to do in order for your child to become happy and productive in the classroom. This may be because the teacher is unable to make the necessary changes due to either a lack of knowledge on how to make appropriate accommodations for a brilliant child, or to an administration that is too inflexible to allow for certain specific curriculum modifications. Occasionally, however, the problem is not that the teacher is unable, but that he or she is unwilling to make changes—sometimes even simple ones—that would help your brilliant child shine.

Knowing the chain of command in a school district is important if things get tough. You always want to start with the child's teacher. Often, problems can be solved at the lowest level by just working with the teacher, talking together about options for your child, and discussing your child's strengths and weak areas. Meeting with the teacher in a non-threatening, informative way can be effective for enacting the change that your child needs. But if it is not, you may have to start working your way up the chain. If repeated attempts at dealing with the teacher still leave you with a frustrated and unhappy child, your next meeting should be with an assistant principal or department head, if the school is large. In a small school that does not have department heads, you can go directly to the principal. If the principal can't or won't help you, go to his or her supervisor. In a large school district, this might be an assistant superintendent. In smaller districts, it may be the superintendent directly. If that doesn't work, you can always go to the school board. Most private schools also have boards.[19]

It is important to follow this chain of command because going directly to the principal or the school board without trying first to solve the problem with the teacher leaves the teacher feeling blindsided about your complaint, and he or she may have a difficult time trusting you or working cooperatively with you for your child in the future. There is no need to alienate anyone. A team approach generally works best.

If you are a parent of an unfortunate youngster who happens to reside in a classroom or school district in which gifted education and curriculum modifications are frowned upon as unnecessary or even elitist, then you have your work cut out for you. Don't let teachers and administrators intimidate you. Every time you go to a meeting, remember this: You know your child better than they do. You need to advocate for your child so that school can be an inspiring experience.

When meeting with administrators about your child, don't be surprised if there are more people from the school at this meeting than you thought would be there. Educators will often meet with one another before they meet with you to get a grasp of the situation and present a united front to try to persuade you to do what they think you should do. Request ahead of time that the school's gifted specialist or gifted coordinator be present, if there is one. You may also want to bring somebody with you to be an extra ear and advocate. If you are concerned that the school may try to manipulate you, bring a friend who is a teacher, a friend who is an attorney, or someone who donates money to the school. You want someone who either speaks their language or can effectively present low-cost and easy-to-implement alternatives. This will level the playing field.

Communication is the key to success. Educators sometimes capitalize on esoteric knowledge, using abbreviations and educational terms that you don't know, or by making things more complicated than they really are. They may try to tell you how they do things and expect that you will find a way to make it work. You need to be prepared to tell them what your child needs and expect *them* to find a way to make it work. When educators start speaking in their own language, don't be reluctant to stop them and ask them to put things into layman's terms. If what they are saying doesn't make sense, make them explain it. If they tell you that something is "the law" or "district policy" or "school policy," stop them and ask them to show you the written law or policy, which every district has on hand somewhere. When my children were in middle school, I was often told that they had to take gym because it was state law. At that time in our state, there was no law regarding this. When I asked school administrators to see the law in writing, they couldn't produce it. I was thus able to negotiate time for drama classes for my kids in place of gym. This made a huge difference for them and kept them engaged in school for years.

The truth is that most educators really don't know all of the laws and rules that govern things like course requirements, instructional time, etc. They simply repeat what they have heard from others in the district. So the simple act of asking to see the law or policy they are quoting can work wonders in getting appropriate classes or programs for your child—and it might help others along the way as well.

Remember, too, the importance of persistence. Most educators will do whatever they can to stop you from bugging them. Teachers and principals do not want to deal with difficult parents, and principals do not want to deal with school superintendents or other supervisors, so they often will accommodate you just to make you go away. The reasoning behind their accommodations is irrelevant; the important thing is to ensure that your child gets an appropriate education.

Does Your Child Have Special Needs?

Although this might sound strange, you may want to consider having your child evaluated to see if she qualifies for an Individualized Education Plan (IEP), which is used to ensure that the rights of an exceptional child are protected. Brilliant children do have special needs, which were subject to protections at one time, but now only children identified as having a learning disability or a disorder have a legal right to these protections. However, in many states, a child can be labeled as learning disabled simply because of a large difference in achievement between academic areas or due to a large gap between potential and achievement—both of which brilliant children often display. Of course, brilliant children can have learning disabilities or disorders just like any other child, and they have a right to interventions that will help them with those issues as well. Young children with simple speech issues, such as a lisp, may also qualify for IEPs.

An IEP is a legal document guaranteeing due process for an appropriate education, and it can help your child receive many different kinds of assistance. For example, in Florida, any child with an IEP can get a voucher to attend a private school. The state will pay the private school the money normally sent to the local public school district. This can amount to $5,000–$11,000 in scholarship money for your child! You can also use the IEP to get extra time for standardized tests, which many brilliant children need, or to get your child moved to more challenging classes in higher grades, such as a fifth grader taking sixth-grade math. For children with disabilities or disorders, the IEP provides for services such as speech therapy, behavioral therapy, or occupational therapy. Optimally, a brilliant child who also has a disability or disorder (often called a *twice-exceptional* child) should receive curriculum modifications in his area of brilliance so that he is appropriately challenged, and also assistance with his area of weakness to help remediate the deficiency.

If you decide that you would like to explore the option of getting an IEP for your child, request that your child be evaluated. The school must comply with your request. However, it is not uncommon for some school leaders to tell you that this process takes more than a year and that it includes something called RTI, which stands for *Response to Interventions*. RTI is supposed to involve rapidly occurring, successive interventions for children who are demonstrating distress in school, designed to get a child back on track and achieving comfortably in the school setting. In reality, many schools use this process as a way to delay the intelligence and achievement testing that would help determine the course of an IEP. Despite what school personnel may say, this kind of testing can happen at the same time as the RTI, so parents don't need to wait to see if the interventions are working before having their child tested, which actually only takes about half a day to do. The RTI and the testing can happen concurrently, but they probably won't unless the parent insists upon it.

Since schools are known to drag their feet during the IEP process, if you want it to go faster, be a pest. Put every request in writing, and insist that the evaluation process of intelligence and achievement testing happen in a timely manner—within 60 days is optimal. Some parents prefer to go through the RTI process without testing to see if some simple interventions might work well enough to help their child. If this is the direction you'd like to go, tell the principal that you want to participate in the RTI, and see if you can negotiate alternative class placements or other accommodations that you think would help your child.

If you want to continue with the process of getting an IEP, and if the school is too slow in testing your child, you have the right to seek an evaluation from an outside provider. Find a psychologist in your area who does this type of testing and whose results will be accepted by the local school district. This is important, because some schools will not accept reports from certain outside providers, so make sure the psychologist you choose is one whose evaluation will be considered. The school district should be able to provide you with a list of acceptable providers. Many private school operators can also give you this information. Some health insurance plans will pay for this service, in the event that the school doesn't.

Once the evaluation is complete, the school will hold a meeting to discuss the results. Do *not* go into this meeting blind. Ask to see a copy of the evaluation before you go. Determine if it makes sense. Do the psychologist's findings match what you know about your child? Is there information in the report that can be helpful? Analyze the information to see if there are things that can help you get what you want for your child. Do you see great variations between the IQ score and achievement test scores? Do you see areas of need that might be translated into accommodations or services for your child? If you need help analyzing this report, find a psychologist or an experienced special education or gifted education teacher who can help. If you don't know any, ask around to find advocates in your community, or search online for them.

Before you go into the meeting to review the evaluation, remember the purpose of it. This meeting is to determine if the evaluation will qualify your child for an IEP. If it does, the IEP can be written at that time, or a separate IEP meeting can be scheduled at a later date. Also, think about what will help your child. What do you want?[20] It is important to know this before going to the meeting, and to bring an advocate to assist you and to level the playing field, if you can. If you don't agree with the findings on the report, you have the right to get an outside provider to do a second evaluation, at no cost to you. If you accept the report, think about what you want to do with the information. What things do you think should be included in your child's IEP? In other words, what changes would you like to happen to make school the very best it can be for your child? Have a plan in mind before meeting with educators, and don't be afraid to walk away if you don't agree. They can't move forward at this stage without your signature, and you can continue to negotiate for what you want.

A Word about Special Education Placements

It is best to try to keep your child in the mainstream class-room and have the school implement interventions that will allow your child to stay in as "normal" a setting as possible—the "least restrictive environment" is always a better choice for children. The exception to this is if there is a specialized program for gifted and talented students that matches the educational needs of your child. This is not considered a special education placement.

Unless the class is a gifted class, be very careful about agree-ing to place your child in a separate special education classroom for even a few minutes a day. Once you agree to a class placement in a special ed. class, you give the school permission to remove your child from the mainstream setting. The IEP will specify what percentage of the child's time will be spent in the special ed. class, but this time period can be expanded without your permission. The school can't change your child's placement without a new meeting, but they can extend the time the child spends away from the mainstream classroom by simply notifying the parents that this is happening. This can be especially problematic for children with behavioral issues. If your child has behavioral problems, you may want to include "time out" in a counselor's office or a specific behavior plan. But be very wary of any attempts to place your child in a special education class.

Remember, getting an IEP for your child does not mean that the child must be placed in special ed. classrooms. Once the child has an IEP, special education services can be provided right in the regular classroom. For brilliant children, an IEP can make the teacher accountable for providing differentiated services so that the child's educational needs are met—right alongside her average-ability peers.

Important Elements to Consider

Okay, so you now understand what educational options are available in your community and how you can use the IEP process to help meet your child's educational needs. You've learned about the decision-making structure in the school district and how to communicate with educators. Now let's focus on some aspects of education that need to be considered in order to make the best choices for your brilliant child.

Structure

Think about the type of school structure that works best for your brilliant child. How much structure and routine is important? Some children work best with a rigid structure, in which everything happens the same way at the same time every day. They feel comfort in routine, and they dislike change. These children might like schools that require uniforms so there is less to think about when getting ready each morning. However, other students will wither in this type of environment. They enjoy spontaneity, and a school that alters its routine frequently to include special projects and events excites them and stimulates their brains. They feel trapped and smothered if they are asked to wear uniforms or adhere to a structure that is too inflexible.

When you are considering your child's school options, you will want to know just what the structure of the school day is, what students are required to do and wear, and how much flexibility in the curriculum is allowed. You will also want to know how much movement happens during a typical school day. Does the school offer unstructured time for socialization? How about recess or time for physical activity? Do children work independently or in groups? Talk to your child about each of these issues, and determine what structure will best meet his particular needs as a learner.

Curriculum

When I was the head of a private, independent school in Florida, I was frequently asked by prospective parents: "What curriculum do you use?" I thought that was such a curious question, since curriculum means everything that is taught in a school. What parents were actually wondering usually was: "What textbooks do you use?" A curriculum is not a textbook. A textbook is intended to be a convenient way of providing resources and assignments for students, but it should not be the totality of a curriculum. The greatest learning occurs when teachers are continually improving and adjusting curriculum to respond to changes in culture, knowledge, and student needs.

Here are the some important curriculum terms that you might hear if you discuss this issue with educators:

State standards: These are the learning objectives set by each state for students to meet at certain grades, and they usually form the basis for state-mandated tests. Almost all of our states are now adopting the Common Core State Standards, which is the framework for our national curriculum. Private schools are not required to adhere to the state standards, so if you are talking with people from private schools, you will want to understand how their learning objectives compare to the state standards.

UBD: This stands for *Understanding by Design.* It is a curriculum development process that many schools use to continually develop and improve curriculum. In this process, a teacher or teacher team identifies the end results they are looking for, usually in the form of an "essential question," meaning a "big picture" understanding that students should have when they complete a particular unit or course. For elementary math, this might be something like, "How does multiplication relate to addition?" For a high school social studies class, it might be, "How do the arts influence politics?" Once an essential question is identified, teachers come up with an assessment that will tell them that each student has gained this understanding. The assessment could be a presentation, a paper, a project, a test, or even just a specific type of classroom observation. Once this is identified, the teachers work backward, planning specific activities that will result in the understanding and completion of the assessment. Some teachers refer to this method as *backward design* or *backward planning*.

Thematic instruction: Thematic instruction occurs when several curricular areas are combined around a specific topic or theme. A school might emphasize a certain era in history, learning the scientific discoveries of the time, the political structures, and the arts and literature popular during that era. Or it may use a specific type of statistical analysis across social studies, science, and math classes. You can see thematic instruction in very simple forms in preschool classrooms when children have a "green day" or an "orange day." The idea is to connect learning in a natural way across the areas that schools tend to separate. This can also be called *interdisciplinary study*. Generally speaking, the more connected the curriculum is, the more students will learn.

Textbooks: These are generally large books that give kids sore backs when they have to carry them home. Most public schools have a state-adopted textbook for every class. Private schools vary. A textbook represents what the state deems necessary for students to study for each course. Textbook adoption tends to be a very political process, leading to good or bad results. Don't be alarmed if your child's school uses other materials to supplement, or even replace, the textbooks; students don't really need textbooks in order to learn. But when teachers do use them, be sure your child understands how to use the book and what is expected in terms of work completion.

Assessment: This is probably the most misunderstood term in education today. Assessment simply means what we do, or what instrument or process we use, to determine what a child knows and is able to do. It could be a state-mandated standardized test, but it usually isn't. Assessments can be classroom observations, parent observations, peer observations, specific assignments, projects, performances, presentations, written tests, etc. Educators also sometimes use the terms *formative assessment* and *summative assessment*. A formative assessment is one that is done in the middle of a unit or course to help the teacher understand the progress a student is making so that necessary adjustments in instruction can be made. The summative assessment occurs at the end of the unit or course to see the sum of the learning that took place.

Standardized tests: These are tests that are given in a prescribed, standardized manner so that testing conditions and scoring are consistent. Scores can be reported as raw scores (indicating the number of right and wrong answers) or as standard scores (percentile standing within a normal bell-shaped curve).

High-stakes test: This is any test that has significant consequences for the students taking it or for the schools or school districts they attend. Any test that determines whether a child will advance to the next grade or graduate is a high-stakes test. Any test that results in a rating for a teacher, school, school district, or state is also a high-stakes test.

Constructivism: A constructivist curriculum takes into account the learners' needs and desire to learn. According to educator Audrey Gray,[21] the characteristics of a constructivist classroom are: (1) the learners are actively involved, (2) the environment is democratic, (3) the activities are interactive and student-centered, and (4) the teacher facilitates a process of learning in which students are encouraged to be responsible and autonomous.

Montessori: A Montessori school is a type of constructivist school named for Italian pediatrician Maria Montessori at the beginning of the 20th century. Montessori schools pay careful attention to children's developmental needs, and they structure an environment that allows children to do what they are ready to do when they are ready to do it. Teachers are taught to stay on the sidelines, allowing learners to become self-motivated and self-initiating.

Progressive education: Schools that are progressive lean more toward group activities and experiences than the more traditional methods involving individual assignments and tests. Generally speaking, the more the students work together to solve problems, the more progressive a school is.

Bilingual education: A bilingual school or classroom is one in which students and teachers work in two different languages. The most common type in the United States involves Spanish and English. These programs are effective in teaching students a second language if instituted at a young age.

Instructional Time

The use of instructional time is an important consideration for brilliant children. How is each day chunked? Do students get long stretches of time to work on specific topics or subjects? How frequent are transitions from activity to activity, or class to class? How much of the day is spent at desks or tables? How much do children get to move around? Is there recess or time for physical activity? Are there times when students can socialize? Some children do better with fewer transitions, while others like to switch activities more frequently. Warriors, for example, need more opportunities for large-motor activities. Explorers need longer periods of time to explore and understand a problem. You should think about your child's specific needs and ensure that the school, class, or program can meet those needs.

Teachers

Perhaps the most important element of your child's education is the individual teachers who will be working with her. Even when a school is unyielding when asked to accommodate a child, the right teacher can find a way to make it happen. Conversely, a teacher can prevent needed and mandated changes from occurring. I can tell you that teachers generally do *not* respond well when parents come in armed with research and information on their precious, brilliant child's needs. I have seen this over and over again. Many books and experts advise parents to bring teachers information about what will help their child, but this can be insulting or threatening to a teacher, who is supposed to be the educational expert. What helps the most is the most basic approach. Establish a relationship with your child's teacher. Get to know her or him as a human being. When you have a conversation about your child, start with phrases like, "I am concerned about him because..." or, "I am not sure she is engaging in...." Talk about what is troubling you, person to person. Then ask the teacher if she might have some suggestions. Offer her solutions that work at home. Ask her what her thoughts are on possibilities like altering the schedule, accelerating lessons, etc. Think of this as working together to solve the problem.

However, if this tactic doesn't work, you can use the strategies outlined earlier in this chapter. Before the start of each school year or semester, you will want to think about who might be the best teachers for your child. Who will provide him with the right balance of instructional time? Who will respect him as a learner and help him learn as much as possible? Who will provide just the right type of discipline and responses to your child's behavior? Talk to other parents to learn about specific teachers. Don't be afraid to voice your desires to appropriate school leaders. You may not always get everything you want, but if you make enough noise, the principal will help to pair your child with the most effective teachers, if only to make you leave him or her alone!

Making Education Just Right for Your Child

Think about your child's area of brilliance and how it might impact her educational needs. Here are some factors to consider for each area of brilliance.

Storytellers

Everything revolves around language for Storytellers. They do well in schools or programs where they can explore languages through reading and writing, with longer periods of time to engage in these tasks. They tend to be fairly intellectual and generally respond well to many different types of schools, since most schools are geared toward this type of learner. You will, however, want to ensure that reading materials are at an appropriate level, as Storytellers quickly tune out when mandated to read things that are not engaging enough. Unfortunately, we are in an era when students can be tested nearly to death in schools, which can thwart children's creativity and passion. Many exceptional Storyteller students cannot score better than average on state writing tests, which emphasize formulaic responses to canned prompts. Work with teachers to ensure that your Storyteller gets opportunities to read and write things that are beyond the required curriculum. Think about alternative reading selections that might be more interesting for your child, and teach him to advocate for himself to make these selections. In addition, many Storytellers need a little encouragement to engage in social interactions, so be sure that somebody at the school (peers or teachers) will do so. Bilingual programs and drama are particularly stimulating for this group.

Calculators

Calculators thrive in an orderly, structured environment. They tend to do well in more traditional structures where things are predictable, but they generally need assistance in dealing with change and seeing things globally. Choose schools and programs that have tight structures yet allow children to accelerate in math. These kids need to be pushed forward at warp speed as soon as they master a concept; they get offended when asked to practice a math skill over and over once they have learned it. Unfortunately, most of our schools are set up to teach students a finite set of skills at each grade level and have few opportunities for children to move beyond the basics. Work with teachers and school leaders to help your child gain access to mathematics when she is ready, not just when the curriculum dictates. If the regular classroom doesn't allow for this, consider having your child attend classes in higher grades or take advanced math classes online. Most community colleges provide options for dual enrollment for high school students so they can continue their math education as needed. Don't hold your Calculator back in this area, or you may lose her spark forever.

Explorers

Like Storytellers, Explorers need time to process information and to work on specific projects. They do well in schools with fewer transitions and longer blocks of time in each subject. They need opportunities to ask tons of questions, and they often stump the teacher. This sometimes causes the teacher to resent them and try to shut them down. Consequently, Explorers do infinitely better in more progressive classrooms that include constructivist and Montessori approaches. If you can't get that for your Explorer, teach her some strategies to help her get along in the regular classroom. Ask her to write all of her questions down and talk with the teacher after the formal lesson has concluded. Teach her to advocate for herself to include some discovery in classroom assignments. Ask about programs like Odyssey of the Mind and Future Problem Solving for her, which can be a good way to bring problem solving and an integrated curriculum into the classroom environment.

Magnets

Magnets need opportunities to lead. Like Explorers, Magnets do best in more progressive schools where lots of group interaction is occurring. However, they sometimes get frustrated when they are responsible for a group's performance, so make sure that teachers grade students individually and not as a group, even for group projects. Magnets like to join clubs and sports teams where they can function as leaders or captains. They also enjoy interacting with adults on a much different level than their same-age peers. Be sure you help your Magnet understand how he can satisfy this need to lead other students and engage with adults in a way that will not be offensive to others. Talk to him daily about his interactions, and help him work through any issues that may arise.

Designers

Designers see the world as one big art project, so when you are touring a potential school for your Designer, look for art. Is it everywhere, woven into the fabric of the school? Or is it only present in the art room? You want a school that has a strong art program *and* an integration of art into the entire life of the school. Also, pay attention to the artwork that you do see. Do all of the pieces look the same or similar? If so, this school may not be the best fit for your child. Designers need to be able to express themselves in an individual manner, so you should be looking for indicators of individuality in student work. The school should also show clear signs that it values student expression. Schools that require uniforms are not the best choice for Designers. Designers who attend these schools usually challenge the dress code in every way possible, causing continual friction with administrators and faculty. You should also look for evidence that teachers in the school seek out the voices of all of the children. Since Designers are often quiet and introspective, they tend to do better in environments where they can interact with their peers in smaller groups, where all voices are heard and valued. Finally, Designers learn best when lessons are presented with pictures and maps, and they usually benefit from graphic organizers and pictorial representations of concepts and ideas. Teach your Designer how to advocate for himself to use these types of approaches in the classroom.

Melody Makers

Young musicians sometimes have difficulty in schools where everything is focused on reading and writing. These children must have access to music in order to thrive, so be sure that your Melody Maker has opportunities to experience music in school. A twice-per-week "special" music class is simply not enough. Ideally, music should be everywhere in a school for your Melody Maker. In addition to band and chorus, look for evidence that music is integrated into academic lessons. Do teachers play music in the background during independent work time? Are there options for using music in individual or group work? When teaching history, do teachers include the music of the era and culture that the students are studying? Can students write or play music to show what they understand? Do teachers play music to mark transitions in activities? Your Melody Maker will thrive in a learning environment that uses music and sound. Help her advocate for herself to use music in assignments whenever possible. If students are required to give presentations, consider with her how to make them musical. Help her understand how to use raps, songs, and rhymes to memorize things. Melody Makers do not flourish in silent environments. They need the stimulation of productive sound. Listen in each classroom and in common spaces for music and other sounds that provide evidence that sound is valued.

Butterflies

Butterflies need to move. They are kinesthetic learners who retain knowledge best when it involves some type of physical movement. For example, in reading, they benefit from tracing letters and words with their fingers to make that physical connection. As you tour a potential school for your Butterfly, pay attention to how space is organized. Are students arranged in neat rows in every room? If so, this may not be the best fit for your child. Look for classrooms where there are several different types of learning spaces for children. Can students work on the floor or in more comfortable chairs, like rockers, balls, or bean bags? Is there open space outside of the traditional classroom where small groups or individuals can migrate to work on projects? Look for spaces that allow for student movement to ensure that your Butterfly will have room to roam. Similarly, watch children moving through the halls and in common spaces. If they are forced to walk in tight lines like soldiers or robots, this may not be a good place for your Butterfly. But if you notice that children are bopping along in looser lines or no lines at all, you can rest assured that teachers are encouraged to let students behave more naturally, embracing their physical energy. You will also want to know how student learning is assessed at your Butterfly's school.

Can students do things to demonstrate understanding that allow for kinesthetic expression, or is everything related to paper-and-pencil expression? Your Butterfly needs a place where movement is valued and used to ensure that learning is occurring.

Charmers

Charmers want to be the center of attention all the time. They need to be in a school or classroom that values class presentations and allows them to capitalize on this aspect of their personality. Charmers enjoy being in the "star" position on sports teams, in the arts, and in small groups in the classroom. They do well in all types of educational settings, as long as they have enough attention. Look for schools with small class sizes and opportunities for your Charmer to be the center of attention, along with the guidance he needs to keep his feet on the ground.

Warriors

Warriors need to move, and they thrive in schools that honor their physiology by including time for play and learning activities that encourage them to roll around on the floor, jump, and run. If your Warrior's teacher isn't doing this, work with him or her to see if physical activity can be integrated into classroom lessons. In contrast, Warriors need non-physical activities in very small doses. Reading and writing are usually a challenge for them. Teachers are most successful with these students when they chunk assignments into smaller pieces, interspersed with opportunities to move. As discussed for Butterflies, when searching for a school for your Warrior, you should look for classrooms where there are different kinds of learning spaces available so that students can move to different areas to work on projects, preferably on rugs on the floor or in bean bags or comfy chairs. Children should also have some freedom of movement when walking down hallways; if you see them in loose lines or no lines at all instead of tight, straight lines, then you know that teachers are allowing the students to embrace their physical energy. Also, be sure your Warrior's school has recess every day so he can blow off some steam as needed.

How Do You Know if the School Is the Right Match?

The answer to this question is deceptively simple. Is your child happy at school and engaged in real learning that is challenging? Many parents have the misconception that school is something to be endured, that learning is tough and a chore. That just isn't true. If your child is excited to get up and go to school most mornings, and she comes home with stories about fun things she did during the day and new things she has learned, chances are that things are pretty good.

Many parents get caught up in comparing standardized tests scores and grades. Instead of relying only on formal data, it is important that you understand your child's school experience and whether it is meeting her need for relevance and engagement. You can find out by using this script for your daily after-school discussions:

- ✔ *Tell me something funny that happened today.*
- ✔ *Tell me something new that you learned today.*
- ✔ *What did you read at school today?*
- ✔ *What did you write at school today?*
- ✔ *What other kids did you work with today? Play with today?*
- ✔ *What adult helped you today?*

By asking these specific questions, you will help your child understand that you are interested in what he is learning and who he spends time with. His answers will lead to meaningful dialogue about what is important and how he is really spending his time. Don't worry about asking about challenges and difficulties. These will come up naturally as part of the conversation. Pay attention to his mood as he discusses each topic to ensure that he is finding school to be a meaningful experience that is inspiring him to learn. If he has that, you really don't need to worry about much else. Children who are engaged at school and are happy there will continue to learn and grow.

CHAPTER 5

Light and Shadow: Uneven Development in Brilliant Children

Perhaps the biggest challenge that accompanies each area of brilliance is frustration with other areas of development that may be more typical. This is called asynchronous development, and it occurs when an area of brilliance is far ahead of other areas of ability. Although a child may have amazing abilities in some areas, she may be "only average" or even a complete blunderer in others. This can cause feelings of failure, when in fact the child is quite successful.

In addition, brilliant children tend to have great intensity regarding their area of brilliance, typically exhibiting heightened energy levels and a drive to mastery. So when a child who is brilliant in one area finds herself average or even below average in another, feelings of inadequacy and a sense of urgency to gain competence can be overwhelming.

Understanding the frustrations of brilliance requires you to understand a little bit about child development. Children generally develop their ability to walk about the same time they can talk, and most often, a child's physical development occurs in synch with the cognitive abilities necessary to manage new mobility and skills. But what happens when some skills develop early? For example, what about the young Storyteller who wants to write a story that she has created but who cannot adequately manipulate a pencil to actually write the words? How can a young Calculator who is capable of doing advanced math in the early elementary years possibly endure lessons in counting and adding? Asynchronous development is common among brilliant children, particularly those at the highest levels of giftedness,[22] and it can make a child feel out of step within herself and with her peers.

When my son Daniel was in middle school, he was working on a project for school that involved cutting and pasting images to create a visual display. It was a typical middle school presentation in the days before PowerPoint and the Internet. Daniel sat at the kitchen table for more than an hour attempting to cut out the images in the way he wanted them, frequently shouting and grunting in extreme frustration. I offered to help, but he refused. Finally, I insisted that he allow me to cut out the pictures for him. He was embarrassed and angry that at age 12, he didn't have the physical dexterity necessary to handle this simple task. It didn't matter to him that the content of his presentation was extremely advanced. At that moment, it meant nothing to him that his reading and writing skills were at a college level. He just wanted to be able to use a pair of scissors. This is the curse of asynchronous development—brilliant in one area and much less able in others. Parents and teachers can assist these children by helping them to strengthen their weaker areas so that they can feel competent enough to use their brilliance.

In our case, after the event with the scissors, my husband decided that our son needed to learn to play guitar to help him develop his fine-motor skills. Daniel loved music and was really into indie rock at the time. So we bought him an electric guitar and enrolled him in lessons. It was slow going at first, but thanks to an amazing teacher, Daniel was able to master the guitar. Eventually, he also learned to play the bass, and he still plays in a band as an adult, just for fun. We could have enrolled Daniel in occupational therapy, but instead, we chose to engage him in something that would focus on his interests and make the development of his fine-motor skills fun and motivating. As his fingers grew stronger and more able to handle simple tasks like cutting and pasting, his frustration lessened, and he was able to enjoy learning again.

Strategies for Evening Out Skills

By this point, you have more than likely identified your child's area(s) of brilliance, and you probably also have a sense of areas that are weaker or where there are deficits. But don't worry too much about a particular area that doesn't seem as strong as the others unless your child expresses frustration or teachers seemed concerned. For example, if your child begins talking at nine months of age but still isn't walking by 13 months, you might find yourself concerned. You may wonder how it could be that a child who is such a rapid learner of words could be so delayed in physical milestones. But this is not terribly unusual for brilliant children. Before you begin to worry, ask yourself some questions. Has this child completed milestones leading up to walking, such as crawling, pulling herself up, and cruising the furniture? If the answer is yes, then she is likely just taking a bit longer to walk. This may be because she is so intently focused on language—to the exclusion of other activities or interests. As your child moves through each stage of development, keep each area in perspective. If the child becomes frustrated by a lack of progress or if you don't see even hints of development, then you may want to explore the issue further.

You certainly should be concerned if your child is losing abilities in areas that were previously developing—for example, a child who was making eye contact and babbling is now looking off into space when you try to engage him. This could indicate a very serious issue. If there is a problem, you want to address it as early as possible, since it is much easier to remediate learning issues while the brain is still developing.

However, most brilliant children are simply asynchronous in their development, and the skills that aren't as advanced as their area(s) of brilliance seem so much slower to them by comparison. This can lead to mood swings and frustration. Watch for these in your brilliant child, and see what might be causing them. Common areas of frustration for brilliant children include:

- ✔ *Communication skills:* speaking, listening, making eye contact, expressing emotion, making wants and needs known

- ✔ *Large- (gross-) motor skills:* crawling, walking, running, hopping, skipping, throwing and catching large objects, riding tricycles and bicycles, swimming

- ✔ *Small- (fine-) motor skills:* grasping small objects, using writing implements and eating utensils, dressing and undressing, using scissors

- ✔ *Social interaction:* reading facial expressions and responding, making eye contact, parallel play and later playing with others, working in collaborative groups, making and keeping friends

The rest of this chapter contains specific advice to parents to help their brilliant children strengthen these areas.

Communication Skills

Storytellers have a great advantage in communication and usually excel in their ability to express their ideas and emotions. But children with other areas of brilliance are frequently frustrated by their lack of ability to help others understand all of their big ideas. Explorers can struggle mightily with this and sometimes become angry at others who cannot understand their questions or what they are attempting to learn. Warriors can be very emotional when they experience triumph or loss in their endeavors, and many are not quite sure how to express those emotions. So how can you assist a child who is experiencing frustration in communicating her big ideas or strong emotions to others?

If you are the parent of a brilliant child, it is important that you understand what typical development looks like. A list of key developmental milestones follows so that you will have a good frame of reference.

Development Check

Communication is an ongoing process. Long before speech develops, babies begin communicating. They make eye contact, smile, babble, and listen intently. Most children begin saying a few words around their first birthday. The ability to speak in short sentences emerges by age one and half or two. By about age two, children should be able to communicate their wants and needs with words. By age three, they are generally able to describe people, places, and things. Sometime between their third and fourth birthdays, they are able to carry on simple conversations by asking and answering questions from other children and adults. By age five, most children can communicate more complex ideas and are able to carry on sustained conversations.

Strategies for Success

Drawing is a simple but effective way to help your child communicate. Have him draw pictures of what he is trying to tell you or what has happened that he would like to talk about but can't seem to explain. Once the picture is complete, ask him to tell you about it. See if you can assist him in finding the words to match what he is feeling and trying to say.

Musical expression is another way to communicate thoughts and emotions. Ask your child if he can think of a song that matches what he is feeling. Listen to the song together, and discuss how it expresses his thoughts at the moment.

Role play is another strategy that can be helpful for children who need help learning to express themselves, particularly when it comes to emotional issues. If your child has frequent misunderstandings with classmates, you may want to reenact an event and give your child the opportunity for a "do over." Or you may want him to play the other person to help him develop more empathy and understanding of how his communication is being received.

Use "I" statements, and teach your child to use them when he is trying to communicate his emotions or needs. Give him a script like, "I need you to understand that…," "I am wondering about…," "I am hoping you will…," etc. When frustration is high, we tend to point our fingers at others and say, "You are…," or, "You are not…." So instead of your child saying, "You are not listening to me," teach him to say, "I need you to listen to me." Or instead of saying, "You have to do it like this," say, "I need you to do it this way." Teach him that the first step in the effective communication of strong emotions or needs is to set his expectations for the conversation or activity.

When your child is trying to talk with you, be sure to give him your undivided attention. Effective communication is only possible when we really listen to what the other person is saying. Set some ground rules in your family about paying attention to one another. When your child needs to talk, get rid of all distractions, like phones, televisions, and computers. Focus completely on your child, and insist that he focus completely on you. Talk about this expectation, and help him find gentle ways to insist on the undivided attention of others with whom he is attempting to communicate.

A note about adolescent and pre-adolescent children: Many girls and some boys in this age bracket exhibit the "flight" response when asked to communicate their feelings. We see this most commonly in ninth-grade girls, but signs of it are usually evident much earlier. If your teenage girl has a tendency to roll her eyes, she is also likely to turn on her heels and run as soon as she is confronted with a difficult conversation. Don't let her do this. Insist that she stay and talk calmly with you about issues. Be adamant that she make appropriate eye contact and not roll her eyes. Make her engage fully in the conversation, even when she would rather do other things.

Not every conversation needs to be a serious one, however. Many of the best conversations happen naturally. Work on a fun or interesting project with your child, and spend quality time together while you are doing it. You might bake cookies together, or work in the garden, or even organize a closet or garage. Engaging in this type of team work often opens the lines of communication. While you are working, ask non-threatening questions to get your child to open up to you. Sometimes taking the focus off of the area of difficulty can help children relax, allowing their words to flow more freely.

Large- or Gross-Motor Skills

Large-motor skills, also called gross-motor skills, include things we do with our whole bodies. For children, this means movements like walking, running, and riding a bicycle. These basic skills are reflected in playground games, sports, and outdoor play. Children who struggle with delayed development in this area can often feel left out because so much of a young child's social world revolves around large-motor activities. Opportunities for developing large-motor skills have become more limited in recent years, so it is critical that parents pay close attention to their child's development in this area. While normally a strength for Warriors and Butterflies, large-motor skills can be a particular challenge for Melody Makers and Storytellers.

Development Check

The development of large-motor skills can be seen through developmental milestones like sitting up, crawling, and walking. Generally, we expect babies to be able to sit up without support between six and eight months of age. Soon after that, at around eight to 10 months, they begin crawling. Once they are crawling, they soon start to pull themselves up on the furniture and "cruise." They enjoy this new mobility and quickly start taking steps on their own. This usually happens at around one year of age. It doesn't take long before walking turns into running and jumping, and by about a year and a half, it is tough to keep up with them!

Children between the ages of one and two years are accidents waiting to happen, as their brains struggle to keep up with their bodies. During this time, they enjoy pushing toys designed for this purpose and riding toys with wheels that allow them to propel themselves by pushing along the floor with their feet. They begin to start riding tricycles with pedals at around age three, and they are capable of using bicycles by about age five. Some require training wheels to start using bikes, while others just hop on and ride. The ability to swim actual strokes like freestyle (also known as the crawl stroke) occurs at around the same time a child can ride a bike. Also by this time, most children are able to throw and catch a large playground ball and can kick. This allows them to participate in playground games like kickball and in sports like soccer. Many children get involved in T-ball at this age and develop skills using smaller-sized balls rather quickly. By about age eight, most children can engage in almost any of the typical team sports, such as baseball, touch football, basketball, and soccer.

Strategies for Success

So what if your child just doesn't seem to be able to keep up? There are two very important motivators for the development of large-motor skills: peer pressure and interest. Most children want to be able to do what other kids can do. When they see their younger siblings doing things that they have not yet mastered, they particularly want to be able to do those things. Be sure your child has plenty of opportunities to witness other children doing developmentally appropriate activities. Talk about the fun that comes along with participating in these activities, and encourage your child to take part. If she is shy about playing with other children her age or embarrassed about her lack of skills, put together a "safe" group of friends and family members to help her learn.

Make play a part of your daily routine. Go into the yard or to the park every day and engage in physical activity with your child, like kicking around a ball. If you can't get outside, use indoor-friendly balls and toys that encourage the development of gross-motor skills. Examples for toddlers are push and riding toys. Older children needs bikes and sporting equipment. Develop a daily ritual of whole-body physical activity right before dinner. You might even make it a fun, competitive event. My sisters and cousins and I always included balloon volleyball in our festivities when we couldn't get outside. Just remember to use age-appropriate toys and to stay away from motorized car replicas or other toys that reduce the need for children to propel themselves.

Encourage your child to walk at every opportunity. If your child is older than three and you are still dragging a stroller to the mall, you are thwarting her development. By this age, she should be walking and running everywhere, with little (if any) time in a stroller. Take her to interesting play areas where there are new physical challenges to be mastered. There are many outdoor and indoor spaces with amazing things to climb on, jump off of, and hang from. Don't just go to the same one all the time; find new ones to keep interests high, and then get out of the way so your child can explore. Consider natural challenges like hiking in parks or bike riding on off-road trails that might be of interest to your child. Explorers especially love this![23]

As your child gets older, think about activities that might be really interesting to her. Pay attention to what she thinks is cool, and then give her access to these activities. You can also share your love for particular sports and activities with your child. If you are a swimmer, take her to the pool with you. If you like to ski, put her on the slopes with you. Encourage, share, and provide access to multiple activities so that your child can develop the skills she needs to keep up with her peers.

Small- or Fine-Motor Skills

Small-motor skills, also called fine-motor skills, involve everything we do with our hands. This includes activities like using a pair of scissors, brushing teeth, picking up small objects, writing, or drawing. Children who have not mastered basic fine-motor skills quickly become frustrated and sometimes completely shut down at school or at home. They may have tantrums, sob, or refuse to engage in tasks that they are asked to do.

Development Check

Babies begin batting at objects in front of them sometime around three months of age. Between four and eight months, they typically begin picking up large objects with both hands. At about eight or nine months, they become able to grasp and hold smaller objects with one hand. At about the time of their first birthday, they begin holding large crayons and pencils and are able to move them across paper. Fine-motor skills then gradually increase, and by the time children are about three, they can draw discernible shapes. Sometime between ages four and five, they begin to write letters and even words. Children are usually able to use scissors and successfully cut and paste between the ages of five and six.

Strategies for Success

What if you have a child like my son, who is seldom able to successfully execute a specific task like cutting and pasting? You will want to engage him in interesting activities that improve both strength and coordination. Learning to play a musical instrument can work wonders. Many video games are also helpful in this process and are highly motivating to most children. However, be aware that video games can be nearly addictive to some children, and they may want to play them to the exclusion of all other activities. Your child needs a healthy balance of other types of activities to engage in. Think about sports that utilize smaller muscle groups or promote eye-hand coordination, such as billiard or racquet sports. Involve your child in household chores that require these skills, such as cooking, gardening, or doing the dishes. Think about what would be interesting for your child, and then create lots of opportunities for him to engage in activities that will build strength and coordination in his hands.

Social Interaction

Your child's ability to interact successfully with peers will color every aspect of her life. You want to be sure that she will be able to enjoy the company of others and form meaningful relationships that can sustain her throughout her life.

Development Check

Babies begin life by forming bonds with their parents and others who are part of their lives. This starts with the simple act of making eye contact during feeding or when parents talk to them. Infants should be able to sustain this type of eye contact within one or two months after birth. As babies grow, they start to notice other babies around them. Sometime between their first and second birthdays, children typically begin engaging in what is referred to as parallel play. This means that they play next to each other, aware of the other child's presence, but not really interacting. By the time a toddler turns two, he will likely begin reaching out to other children, offering them things or taking things from them. His skills in interacting and playing with other children will gradually improve so that sometime between the ages of four and five, he will be able to take turns, role play, and engage in simple games with other children his age. During the elementary school years, children continue to develop their social skills, learning how to have conversations with other children, participate in cooperative learning groups, and just enjoying the company of their peers. When adolescence kicks in, kids learn even more complex social skills and begin to discover romantic attractions to others.

Strategies for Success

Social skills can be challenging for many brilliant children to master. Even Magnets and Charmers may find it difficult to have meaningful relationships with others. They may be overzealous in engaging in social situations and find difficulty establishing deeper, more meaningful relationships.

You can assist your child in engaging socially by providing some intentional guidance. Provide plenty of opportunities for your child to interact with others through structured and non-structured activities that capitalize on her strengths. Some children do not instinctively know how to approach other children when they play. You may have to teach your child what to say and do when she encounters different situations. You can do this by role playing situations before or after they occur and talking about alternative ways of handling things. Once your child begins interacting with peers, talk to her about what a friend is, and discuss what good friends do and don't do.

Structured groups and activities are great places for your child to try out new social skills. You may want to talk with adult leaders ahead of time and ask them to assist your child with some explicit instructions for social interaction in case she seems lost. Think about what she likes the most, ideally related to her area of brilliance, and find a group setting that will provide her with opportunities to interact with others.

You will also want to provide some unstructured social activities for your child. Set up a pizza party at your house. Take her and a few friends to the movies or bowling or to a park so they can play together. Stand back and watch how she does. If she seems like she needs a little assistance, find a way to casually take her off to the side and give her some coaching. After the outing, talk with her about what went well and how she can improve. With just a little encouragement, most children can master basic social skills quickly.

Teach your child how to be polite. When she has a friend over, say, "Thank you for coming." When the friend leaves, say, "I had a nice time." If she is the guest, teach her to say things like, "Thank you for inviting me."

When your child meets someone new, instruct her on how to make appropriate eye contact and to say, "Hello, I'm Morgan," or, "I'm happy to meet you." Teach her to say, "Excuse me…" and to not interrupt when others are speaking. A few simple courtesies go a long way toward improving social skills.

Uniqueness

Every human being is unique, with strengths in some areas and relative weaknesses in others. By celebrating your child's areas of brilliance and helping to even out development in other areas, you can help him become a truly wonderful, successful adult.

CHAPTER 6

The Kaleidoscope: How Relationships Reflect and Influence Brilliance

A kaleidoscope contains a circle of mirrors that create multiple reflections. Many of us remember from childhood a toy kaleidoscope that produced a beautiful array of colors and designs when you looked into it and turned it around in your hands. A child's peer relationships form a kind of kaleidoscope, allowing one friend's image to reflect off of another, and then another as they influence each other's behaviors and decisions. Together, the child's "crowd" will create an image unto itself.

Children can be part of a "good" crowd or a "bad" crowd. A brilliant child's kaleidoscope of friends either will encourage and reflect brilliance or will dissuade the child from displaying that brilliance in an effort to be more "normal" or more "cool," which can have the tragic result of the brilliance going dark. As a parent, you need to watch your child's kaleidoscope of friends closely and intervene whenever it becomes detrimental.

Unfortunately, brilliant children often feel like outsiders—just slightly out of step with their peers. Many prefer the company of adults or children who are much older than they are. These are their intellectual peers—those individuals who may not be like them in chronological age, but who are instead like them in intellectual or academic or creative pursuits. It is important for brilliant children to have these kinds of peers with whom they can truly connect. The best possible scenario, of course, is for a brilliant child to find intellectual peers who are also age peers. These "kindred spirits" can form intense relationships that in many cases last a lifetime.

There are times when a parent does nothing to encourage a brilliant child to explore relationships with others his own age or with intellectual peers because the parent is trying to protect the child from rejection, or the parent enjoys the child's company and wants to keep him all to herself. While this may seem preferable at the time, it robs the child of opportunities to create his own kaleidoscope—and a lifetime of meaningful relationships.

When I was a freshman in high school, I had serious challenges in the area of social development. I enjoyed being home and talking with my parents and their friends. I also liked reading (a solitary activity) and generally keeping to myself. Although I had previously been involved in extracurricular activities, I had recently moved to a new community that lacked some of the things I had enjoyed when I was younger. So I just stayed home. Thankfully, my mom realized that I needed to get out of the house and learn to relate to my peers. Well, maybe she was just anxious to get me out of the house.

One Friday night, she overheard me saying something to my sisters about a party, and she suddenly informed me that I was going. I tried to explain to her how I didn't really fit in, how I would rather just stay home, but she would not take no for an answer. She told me that I had no choice in the matter, and she forced me to go. So I went, and I felt uncomfortable before I even got to the door. But by the time I turned around to go back to the car, my mom was long gone. All I could see was the dust from her tires rolling down the dark country road. She wasn't coming back for a couple of hours, so I just had to grin and bear it.

That was a very challenging experience for me. I had no idea what to say to those kids. But somehow, with much consternation, I muddled through and figured it out. By the time my mom returned a couple of hours later, I had really enjoyed myself and had actually made a new friend. This is not to say that high school was easy for me from that point forward. I never really fit in the way others did, and I struggled socially in many ways. But I learned how to function, and I eventually made some very good friends who, I am proud to say, are still my friends to this day.

The Importance of Friendships

Friendships are important. As adults, we understand this, but sometimes we forget that the skills we learn as children are what allow us to have friendships into our adulthood. Friends share our joys and our pain. Life without them is lonely indeed.

Your child may express to you that he does not want friends. Many brilliant children, particularly Storytellers and Explorers, prefer to spend their time with books and engage in other solitary activities. They need this alone time; some need more than others. Some people get downright irritable when they don't get enough time to themselves. In contrast, some people crave constant company. As adults, we arrange our lives in part based on this need. The kinds of jobs we have, where we live and with whom, and what we do for fun are all influenced by our need to have (or not to have) human contact.

But even people who like their alone time still need a friend or two. Although is it important for a brilliant child to be able to choose to be alone to think and create, it is altogether different if a child is alone because he cannot seem to make friends. There is a difference between being alone and being lonely. You want to be sure that your child has the ability to establish meaningful relationships with others.

How can you help your brilliant child make this leap into friendships, and eventually romantic relationships? Should you, like my mother, drop him off at a party and speed away? Maybe. But let's start with a slightly more subtle approach. The first thing you want to do is to determine if this is an issue for your child. Many brilliant children, particularly Magnets and Charmers, have a multitude of friends. They just need to learn not to take advantage of them. More on that later. If your child is lucky enough to have a peer group with many similarities, he may not struggle in this area.

By the time children enter kindergarten or first grade, they generally are able to establish friendships and enjoy spending time with same-age peers. As a guide to your child's approach to friendship, consider the following questions:

- *Does your child lack the social skills to interact effectively with peers?*

- *Does your child hide behind books, video games, and other media as way to avoid people?*

- *Does your child go out of his way to avoid just about all social situations?*

- *Is your child frequently excluded from parties or fun events like bowling, shopping, or movies?*

- *Does your child have difficulty identifying two or three children his age whom he can call and invite over to your home?*

If you answered "yes" to any of these questions, your brilliant child likely needs a little support and assistance in developing appropriate social relationships. You can employ some very simple strategies to help him get over his fears and move into the world of relationships.

Helping Children Develop Friendships

As a parent, you need to establish for your child the appropriate norms for social relationships. Talk with your child about how real friends behave, as well as how to select friends. Good friends:

- Talk to each other about their hopes and dreams
- Care about each other and help each other succeed
- Encourage each other to try new things
- Help each other to do the right thing and stay out of trouble

✔ Lean on each other when the going gets tough

✔ Are kind to one another and try to be inclusive of others

Set an expectation for your child to develop at least one friendship with a child close to her age. You can do this by following these simple steps:

✔ Discuss the definition of a friend.

✔ Make a list of all of the children your child currently has contact with in school, through community organizations, or in the neighborhood.

✔ Determine which of these children your child believes would fit the criteria of a friend.

✔ Discuss what she likes about those children.

✔ Decide upon a few of those children that she would like to spend time with.

✔ Think of natural ways that your child might connect with these children. Can you host a small get-together at your home? Are there projects they might work on together? Are you friends with any of their parents, allowing for family activities together?

✔ Role play how your child might approach each of the children so that she can feel more comfortable doing so.

✔ Discuss what aspects of your child the potential friends might like about her, as well as what traits others might not like. For example, if your child is very competitive, you might want her to practice being a good sport when playing a board game. Think in advance about the things that have derailed social events in the past for her, and assist her in making the necessary adjustments so that these mistakes will not be repeated.*

✔ Debrief your child after she makes attempts at approaching other children so you can assist her in making appropriate behavioral adjustments.

*Note: If your child is on the autism spectrum, you should consult with teachers, behavior specialists, or other professionals who are assisting your child with developing social skills.

Sometimes Intensity Gets in the Way

Brilliant children tend to have intense personalities—not always outgoing, but usually intense.[24] They feel things more deeply, and they can really beat themselves up over small mistakes. They sometimes read too much into minor interactions. When trying to establish new friendships, or even just in maintaining friendships, they can sometimes try too hard and overanalyze every sentence or gesture. You may have to help your intense child calm down and let things happen a little more naturally.

To help your child in his efforts to build friendships and socialize, make your home the place where kids want to congregate after school and on weekends. Think about what might draw other children to your house. Swimming pools, pool and ping pong tables, large TVs with the latest games, etc., are all attractive to kids. But the most important thing is to provide an environment where children feel comfortable, safe, and have just enough room to be themselves. Make your home the "hangout." Provide snacks, and assist your child in inviting other kids over to enjoy them. Once the children are there, you can model appropriate conversations about common interests and events that are happening in school. Then, make yourself scarce so that your child can feel more independent and comfortable around his peers.

If your child has difficulty inviting others over, consider a movie night. When there is a good movie playing on the big screen, offer to be the designated driver to and from the theater for your child and another, or even for a group of children, and then offer snacks at your house afterward. This kind of facilitation may be all your child needs to get a friendship or two off the ground.

Another way to encourage friendships is to have your child join a club or group that includes children that do not attend your child's school. This is especially important if your child goes to a small school or is homeschooled. Interactions with children whom your child doesn't see every day can be less stressful because relationships outside of those more intense environments can be free of the day-to-day "drama" that usually occurs among groups of peers who are together for large periods of time. Consider youth groups, scouts, music or theatrical groups, science clubs, special programs at local colleges for children with brilliance in certain areas, and more. Find organizations and activities that will allow your child to share common interests with other children.

Technology can also assist your child with communication in ways that are less intense. Instant messaging, social networking sites, and texting can be a godsend to children who struggle with social issues. If your child is reluctant to talk in person or on the phone with other children, you may want to help him access the most current communication technology. Just be sure that your child also has opportunities to personally engage with other children. Social networking is a good way to break the ice for some intense children, but do not allow them to hide behind a computer as a substitute for real, face-to-face interactions.

Maintaining Friendships—or Not

Once your child has begun to develop friendships, you need to watch for signs of the health of those friendships. You want to be sure that the relationships your child has are healthy and pointing her in the right direction. It is not uncommon for brilliant children to "dumb themselves down" to fit in with peers, but in doing so, their grades may plummet as they make a conscious effort to neglect academics so as not to be seen as "geeks" and "nerds." Sometimes brilliant adolescents even find themselves a part of the "wrong crowd" as they pursue ways in which to become "cool" or as they rebel against the popular kids who may have teased them before. You want to ensure that your child's peers are continually a good influence on her. You can now reap even more benefits of establishing your home as the local hangout. Be sure to hang around the kids just long enough to determine what kind of influence they are on your child.

If your child is involved with others who are not headed down a path that is healthy for her, she could easily become involved in activities and behaviors that have grave consequences. Be sure she understands that you hold her accountable for her selection of friends, and for her own behavior. To help her have the greatest chance of success, you must teach her how to select appropriate friends, as well as how to remove herself from them if they start making bad choices.

To get an accurate understanding of who your child's friends are, you need to learn about them by talking with them and asking them key questions. My daughter Alison used to refer to my technique as "the interrogation." This typically occurred over pizza or while we were car pooling to various activities. Alison worried about it, but the truth is that the kids who were being "interrogated" usually enjoyed the process because they knew that I cared. Children usually like it when an adult takes an interest in them—especially over a pizza!

How do you do this? I just asked the kids the same sorts of questions that I would ask people I was meeting at a cocktail party. What do you like to do for fun? Tell me about school. What do you like or dislike about it? What things are you looking forward to? What kind of work do you do (if the peer is old enough for this)? For older adolescents, I also asked what the kids were thinking of doing after they graduated, and how they were preparing. You would be amazed how much you can learn in a brief conversation!

I looked for evidence that the child was engaged in life, had hopes and dreams, and was starting to think about the future. If children have these things going for them, they normally stay out of trouble and are a good influence on your child. However, if their only interest is hanging out at the mall and they don't seem to like anyone or anything, this is a cause for concern. In this case, you need to discuss your impressions with your child. At first, she will probably resist, but she will listen, and in most cases, she will also begin to notice these things herself. Bringing this kind of perspective to your child's awareness can often result in her choosing better friends on her own.

How Does Your Child Meet Your Social Needs?

If your child seems to cling to you and doesn't want to go out much, it is time to ask yourself a question: "Do I depend on my child to meet my own social needs?" This is a common problem, particularly for parents who are single. It is even more difficult when the single parent has only one child. This parent-child duo often comes to depend on each other for friendship and then are reluctant to seek the company of others their own age. To determine if you have fallen into this trap, ask yourself:

✔ *Do I frequently engage in social activities with my child?*
✔ *Does my child refer to me as a friend—or even a "best friend"?*
✔ *Do I share information about my dating life with my child?*
✔ *Do I share adult problems with my child, such as job, money, or other difficulties?*
✔ *Does my child frequently worry about me?*
✔ *Does my child tend to offer parental-like advice to me?*

If you answered "yes" to any of these questions, it may be time to re-establish the boundaries between parent and child. This may not be easy, especially if your child is brilliant and can talk with you in a way that indicates understanding and empathy. Brilliant children, with their advanced verbal and cognitive skills, tend to be good at this, and adults can forget that these youngsters are indeed still children.

You are *not* your child's friend. I repeat, you are *not* your child's friend. I cringe every time an adolescent or younger child refers to her parent as her "best friend." You may be friends on Facebook, but you are not really friends. You are the parent, and you will bring on a whole host of problems if you refer to yourself, or allow your child to refer to you, as her friend. If she does this, correct her, and remind her that you are her parent. There will be times when you have to set limits, discipline her, and make her do things she doesn't want to do. Friends don't do this.

Likewise, do not treat your child as a friend. As a parent, you have to check yourself if you find that you are engaging in conversations with your child about adult problems. This is critical. If you are talking about whom you are dating, whether or not you are getting a raise, pressures at work, etc., you are asking your child, however unconsciously on your part, to shoulder your burdens. Kids do not deserve this. It can be tempting to share adult concerns with a child who, intellectually, seems to understand, but you must remember that even the most brilliant child does not have the wisdom, maturity, or life experience that provide perspective. *Adult problems belong to adults.* You only want to share things about your personal and work life with your child that she has a need to know.

For example, let's say that your company is considering pay cuts for employees. You are worried that your salary will be reduced, which could mean that you might have to cut back on things that you and your son enjoy, such as his music lessons, or even sell your home or take on a second job. If you were confiding in a friend, you would talk about your fears and anxieties regarding this matter. You would discuss your options, and the two of you would sort through potential strategies to take should this occur. Certainly, it is important that you have someone in your life with whom to share this sort of thing. But it can't be your child. If you start talking about these issues and concerns with him, you burden him with potential problems that he is helpless to fix. He can't look at other jobs for you. He can't renegotiate your mortgage or put the house up for sale. He can't go to your boss to ask the tough questions. All he can do is worry. And he *will* worry.

Instead, find a friend or adult family member to help you sort through this issue and come up with solutions. Keep your child out of the conversation until he has a need to know. Once the salary cut actually happens, you might tell him that money is tighter than before and that you will have to come up with some ways to deal with it together. Assure him that you both will be fine. Then, you and he can think of ways to save money, like eating out less often, watching your energy consumption, cutting television service, etc. Tell your child that the goal is to save a certain number of dollars each month, and strategize together how you will reach that goal. This way, your child can contribute to the solution, and he is empowered to help make things better for your family. Children who engage in this type of problem solving with their parents learn important lessons about dealing positively and proactively with difficult situations. Conversely, children who are dragged into adult conversations before any action can be taken, or when they are truly powerless to help, just become anxious and depressed.

Remember, your brilliant child is still just a child. If you have allowed the lines of your relationship to become blurred, you may need to have a conversation with him about your role as a parent and why it is important to maintain that role. Discuss why you want to ensure that he does not confuse you with a friend. Of course you enjoy spending time together, but you are, and will always be, the one who protects him and steers him in the right direction.

Your Social Life

The most important thing for your child to know about your social life is *nothing*. It is really none of her business, and she will just worry if you drag her into it, especially if you are single and dating. Many parents fall into this trap because their children, particularly in the teen years, ask a lot of questions. This especially happens when a parent is preparing for a date. You might be excited and anxious and seek advice from your child on what you are going to wear. She may notice that you are making special efforts to look attractive, but this usually leads her to start thinking about what your new relationship might mean to her. Will you marry this person? Will this person take your attention away from her? Does this person have children? Will she have to have relationships with those children? What is this person like? How will he or she treat her?

Brilliant children tend to be sensitive and can connect ideas quickly. When faced with new family structure possibilities, they engage in long-range planning for their entire future—and yours—even if all you did was ask for an opinion on an outfit for a date. Because of this tendency, it is really best that your child not know where you are going, or with whom. If she asks, be vague. Tell her that you're meeting a friend. If she asks for specifics, gently explain to her that she doesn't need to know everything there is to know about your social life, and that it's okay—even healthy—for you to spend time with people you enjoy. Your child may badger you for more information, particularly if you have previously been open with her about these kinds of details. If this happens, tell her that in the past, you gave her too much information about your social life, and you have since decided this is not something she needs to worry about.

Some parents choose to not prepare for social occasions when their child is present. They arrange for the child to sleep over at a friend's or relative's house so that she won't be a part of the process at all. Remember, you are the parent. You have no obligation to provide your child with details about your social life. If you want your child to develop social interactions with children her own age, you need to set these boundaries.

Romance

Ah, romance. This part of development usually happens when you least expect it—and usually way before you are ready! But your child will certainly one day develop romantic feelings for someone. You will want to assist him in evaluating a romantic partner in much the same way as he evaluates his friends, though this will be difficult if you haven't already established strong communication with him. You will also need to help him consider one additional critical aspect of the relationship: whether or not the potential partner is intellectually compatible with him. While it is possible, and even healthy, for children to have friends of all different levels of intellectual capacity, it is challenging to be romantically involved with someone who does not share your capacity for cognitive thought.

Think about your child's area of brilliance and what kind of romantic partner could potentially impede the development of that area. If your child is a Storyteller, he might benefit from a partner who can hold a good conversation with him and who is a good listener. If your child is a Warrior, it might be especially fun for her to have a partner who enjoys an active life. If your child is an Explorer, he may want to share his life with someone who is inquisitive and shares his wonder about the world. This is not to say that your child can only have a romantic relationship with someone who shares his area of brilliance; it just means that he might be more successful in a romance with someone who "gets" him and what his area of brilliance means.

I have a good friend, Lisa, who is a Designer. She is incredibly bright and sees the world as one large, artistic palette. She married Steve, a man with no particular area of brilliance who is happy just to make enough money to get along and has no real passions in life. There is nothing really wrong with Steve. He works hard, pays his bills, and enjoys fishing on the weekends. He has been a good partner to Lisa, but she is miserable. For their entire marriage, she has wanted to engage in things that feed her Designer soul—painting, decorating, and creating landscape designs. None of these things is a large source of income for her, though, and Lisa was the main caregiver for their children. So every time she wanted to pursue her interests—the things she needed to feel human—Steve stopped her. He calculated how much money he would potentially lose by taking time off to care for the children and then tell Lisa that since her interests did not produce much income, it wasn't practical for her to pursue them. Well, the kids are now out of the house, and Lisa is once again beginning to actively pursue her passions. But she has built up so much resentment toward Steve, who cannot possibly understand her Designer nature, that she now wonders why she ever married him. For Lisa, this mismatch has caused great misery and unfulfilled potential.

You should talk with your brilliant child about the pitfalls of becoming romantically involved with someone who does not share his perceptions of the world, does not support them emotionally, or does not understand them.

Breaking Ties

How do you know if your child is involved in a friendship or romantic relationship that is becoming unhealthy? It's simple. You will see a change in your child's behavior that cannot be explained by normal development or external circumstances. Most importantly, you will see a decrease (usually sudden) in her desire to engage in things that used to give her pleasure, usually related to her area of brilliance. If your Butterfly suddenly stops wanting to go to dance class or no longer flits around the house, something is terribly wrong. If you can't relate this to anything obvious that is going on in the home, or with school or the dance studio, chances are that a relationship is taking its toll. Start paying attention to whom your child is spending time with and communicating with on the phone or computer. Do a little reconnaissance if you have to in order to figure this out.

Usually, the relationship that is causing the problem will be the one that is most intense, involving the most time and communication. Pay attention to what your child is saying about this person and to this person. What is the person trying to get her to do or not do? Ask your child innocent questions about this person, and see if you can get her to invite him or her to your house so you can see them interact together. Carefully observe them from a distance to see if you can figure out what is causing the problem.

If you determine that the relationship is detrimental to your child's well being, don't be afraid to confront her with this information. But be prepared; she will resist your efforts. Simply saying, "You are not going to be friends with her anymore," or, "You can't see him again," will likely *not* be effective. Teens especially find ways around adults' efforts to keep them apart. Instead, find some ways to get your child engaged in activities that don't involve this person, and set some specific expectations for her behavior. For example, if your child is spending hours and hours online, put a limit on it. By limiting her overall screen time, you will be reducing the amount of influence that the friend has over her. If she wants to hang out at the mall, allow that for a specific period of time (a couple of hours on a Saturday), provided that she engages in another activity that she enjoys for the same amount of time that week. Help her find some balance in her life. Continue to expect her to try new activities and experiences so that she is continually meeting new people outside of her current sphere. Then, in a supportive way, point out the things that concern you about the relationship. You may not think she is listening, but she is. Eventually, by using this strategy, she will find her way back to what she loves and not allow an unhealthy relationship to limit her future.

Setting the Context

The relationships your child develops as he grows will create a delightful kaleidoscope through which he will see the world. You want it to be constantly spinning and changing so that he can learn and grow into the person he is meant to be. You want his area of brilliance to continue to shine through it and create new images throughout his life. Teaching him how to develop healthy relationships with people who appreciate and will encourage his areas of brilliance is an incredible gift that you can give him.

Now that you have a good context of peers for your brilliant child, you can focus on helping him to create the discipline necessary to develop his area of brilliance. Read on to learn about how to encourage your child by giving him what he needs to develop his abilities.

CHAPTER 7

The Laser: Focusing In on What Your Child Needs to Develop Brilliance

Discipline, as it relates to work or one's passion, is a dedicated persistence toward mastery. Your child's area of brilliance will only develop through sustained discipline over time. Whether in dance or music, business or law, science or math, academia or a skilled trade, your child will need discipline and hard work to be successful. Your job as a parent is to encourage this self-discipline in a way that inspires and excites. If you make the mistake of pushing, out of fear that your child will never fulfill her potential, she may abandon her pursuit and do something that she considers more fun.

Through recent research,[25] we know that a person can generally only become an expert at a subject or a master of a skill or talent if that person engages in steady, even relentless, pursuit of excellence. So perhaps identifying a child's area of brilliance is more about understanding her true passion for something rather than her innate ability. You can usually tell when someone is passionate about something just by talking to her about it; her face and mannerisms will change; she will be animated. The Designer who explains her latest artistic creation just lights up. The Butterfly can hardly contain himself; he'll be physically moving around, gesturing, perhaps even demonstrating some movement. If you discuss a recent athletic competition with a Warrior, she can barely get the words out due to her intense excitement.

Your job as a parent is to discover the subject that ignites your child and makes her most alive. Then, you need to provide the means—the time, space, tools, and guidance—to allow her to pursue her passion, or multiple passions, for the time it takes for pure mastery. How long will that be? We know now, thanks to the work of K. Anders Ericsson, and later, neurologist Daniel Levitin, that mastery takes 10 years or about 10,000 hours of practice and pursuit. Malcolm Gladwell, in his book *Outliers*, agrees that true expertise comes only after this much practice.[26] It seems that the old "practice, practice, practice" axiom is truer than we thought.

Think about various people you know who are accomplished in a field, and the long years of dedication are probably there. So when you are thinking about areas of brilliance in your child, think about what she might be willing to pursue for 10 years or 10,000 hours. Only a subject that ignites her passion to this degree will be an area worth pursuing. Remember, though, that some children do not discover their area of passion until they are adolescents or adults.

Once you have determined that your child has an area of brilliance, you want to be sure to provide her with all she needs to engage with laser-like focus in this area. Don't worry if she likes other things, too; it is possible for one to enjoy many things in a lifetime—even healthy. But we want to ensure that we are providing just the right blend of encouragement and support for a particular area of brilliance. Your brilliant child needs:

✔ Time and space for the pursuit
✔ Mentors who have already developed mastery in this area
✔ Excited supporters
✔ The necessary tools for the pursuit

✔ Appropriate lessons or other educational aids
✔ The removal of barriers to the pursuit

If your child is fortunate enough to have more than one area of brilliance, she may at some point need to make a conscious decision about which one will get the majority of her focus. She doesn't have to abandon the other completely, but it can be challenging to maintain the level of dedication that will move her forward at the pace she wants in more than one area. It is important to have frank conversations about this issue.

Time

This is probably the most important element of parenting a child with an area of brilliance, and perhaps the most overlooked. In our efforts to give children every advantage, we often over-schedule them into countless lessons, activities, playgroups, and sports. Our children are chauffeured from school to sports field to music school, every day of the week, with barely any free time to breathe and just be kids. When a child is perpetually engaged in highly structured activities, when he is simply following instructions and having to adhere to group norms, he can fail to develop a sense of independence that comes with independent play. Further, when parents are concerned that their child must be enrolled in absolutely everything that is available for fear that they might be denying him of an opportunity, they are actually denying him the opportunity to find the one thing that will fuel his passion and drive him toward mastery. You must think very seriously about how much time you are programming your child into structured activities and how much time you are allowing for him to just be a kid.

Parents should also consider the quality of the activities that their children are enrolled in. The younger the child is, the more varied the activities should be, and the less competitive and rigid. As children get older, they can and should handle increasing levels of competitiveness, whether on the ball field or on the stage. You want them to have to work to become better so that more opportunities will become available to them.

Children need exposure to lots of different things, but not all at the same time. Here are some pointers for different age groups so that you can be sure you are structuring your brilliant child's time wisely.

Ages 2-5

If your child attends school or daycare full time, she doesn't need any other structured activities. Hopefully, she's getting lots of good stuff at school and just needs to play on her own terms during non-school hours. Even if the quality of the structured activities at school is not what you would like it to be, it may not be advisable to add more structured activities for your young child. Resist the temptation of fun activities on top of full-time daycare or school, such as sports leagues, music lessons, or language lessons, at this age. However, if your two- to five-year-old is not in a full-time school-type environment, you may want to join a play group or enroll her in one or two activities that take no more than a few hours a week.

Ages 6-7

You may want to consider starting your six- or seven-year-old in a noncompetitive sports league (just one at a time) that meets no more than a total of three or four hours per week, including all practices and games. This is also a good time to enroll in music or art lessons or language lessons of an hour or so per week. This is a great developmental period for children to learn to play a musical instrument, discover painting and sculpture, or begin to speak a new language. Be sure that the structured time outside of school totals no more than two activities per week for no more than four hours total time per week.

Children who are not used to this amount of unstructured time may require your assistance in learning to make their own fun. Play with them, provide books for them to read, and give them opportunities to create and discover. Be sure to encourage active play and imagination, not simply watching TV or using a computer or playing video games. If your child is in extended school hours due to your work schedule, you don't want anything more than that. If the activities that you want your child involved in happen outside of the extended school day environment, they should *replace* that time, not occur in addition to it.

Be sure that you include sports and the arts in your child's experiences. Parents often only expose their children to what they know or what might be popular among their friends' children. It was sacrilege where my kids grew up to not be in a soccer league. We did involve our children in soccer, but we also included music and theater in their lives from a very early age. This is a time when *you* should be making decisions about what your child should try. Think of activities at this age like vegetables: kids need to be exposed to them and should be encouraged to try them several times before they can decide whether or not they like them. We want to be sure our young children have opportunities to discover what is fun for them.

Ages 8-10

Between the ages of eight and 10, your child should be able to handle a little more time in structured activities, and he may begin expressing interest in certain activities as a result of the exposure you provided him in the previous few years. Continue to expect him to try new things, but be sure that he is involved in only one major activity at a time (one that requires three or more hours per week). Let him choose between two different sports, or two different arts experiences. You should allow no more than six hours of total time in structured activities per week.

Ages 11-13

These are the pre-adolescent years, when you should require even more exposure to new activities if your child has not yet found a passion. If your child has developed a keen interest in something, now is the time to get her really immersed in it. At this point, you can begin looking at time from the opposite perspective, thinking about how much time should be left unstructured. As such, make sure that your child has at least one or two hours of free time per day when she can think and imagine. You will also want to have one full day per week without any structured obligations. This can be a time for you do things together, or she can do things with her friends, without a coach or teacher guiding them. As before, make sure that your child is not involved in more than one competitive sport at a time or major arts activity at a time. Children at this age do not need to be engaged in more than one major commitment at the same time.

Even if your child is involved at this age in an activity of her passion, continue to expect her to try one new thing each year, and to experience at least one sports activity and one arts activity each year. This way you can continue her exploration while still allowing her to develop passion and mastery of one particular talent.

Ages 14-18

Hopefully by this time your teen has found something of great interest to him. You will want to help him pursue his interest by exploring all of the options together. You might find opportunities for him to develop his area of passion in neighboring towns, at local colleges or universities, or through summer camp experiences. Be sure that you still keep some unstructured free time in his schedule, including one large chunk of time per week without any obligations when he can relax. If your teen has not yet found a passion in life, use the guidelines in Chapter 3 to continue his exploration. Look for activities that stress creativity, problem solving, and collaboration. Continue to insist that he try new experiences in athletics and in the arts each year until your high schooler discovers something that excites him.

Overall, your child's daily routine should include the following, at all ages:

✔ A sense of calm, with limits being placed on electronic stimuli

✔ A thoughtful balance of structured activities and free time

✔ A peaceful start and end to each day, made possible by establishing routines and preparing ahead

✔ Good nutrition

✔ A sufficient amount of sleep

By following these guidelines, you can rest assured that you are not pushing too hard toward any particular area of brilliance. Your child will continually be exposed to new things and will be able to determine what is interesting enough to pursue further.

Space

The word *space* means both the physical space and the emotional space for a child to follow her own path. Let's first discuss the physical space. This is often overlooked by well-meaning parents, who underestimate its importance or their ability to change it. You can make space for a child to pursue her area of brilliance even in the tiniest of houses or apartments. As a parent, your most important job is to help your child become a happy, healthy adult. She should feel at home and safe in your house and have space enough to move around and to do the things that fulfill her.

For example, if your child is an Explorer, he may enjoy cooking. Do you allow him to use the kitchen to create things? If you have a Warrior, is there a place for her to run and jump and play? If you don't have a back yard, be sure to give her access to open space, perhaps at a park or playground, every day. You may also want to consider video games that require large muscle movement and can be done safely inside the house. What if you have a Melody Maker who likes to play a loud instrument? Is there a place in your home where he can do that? If not, is there an electronic option with headphones as an alternative? Think about the things your child loves to do—must do—to feel whole. If you don't provide her with the space to do these things, she will quickly become frustrated and angry and may abandon her area of brilliance.

To ensure that you are considering what your child needs, answer the following questions:

- ✔ *What does my child love to do more than anything else?*
- ✔ *Where in our home can she do this?*
- ✔ *If she can't currently do this in our house, what options are there? What can I adjust in the home to accommodate her, or where can I take her on a daily basis so that she can do this?*

The second aspect to consider concerning space for your brilliant child is his emotional space. Parents get into trouble in two different ways in this area. If your child's area of brilliance is similar to your own, you may find yourself pushing too hard, choosing to live vicariously through him. We see this often with Warriors. You may be a dad who was an All-American in high school, but you gave it up for some reason. Now your child shows promise in the same sport, and you are determined not to let him make the same mistake you made. If you find yourself thinking in this way, you may fall into the trap of pushing too hard. Your Warrior will likely begin to resent you and will limit his involvement in the sport to reduce the amount of pressure you are putting on him. You must give him the space he needs to determine what is right for him. These are *his* glory days, not yours!

Similarly, you may wish, for example, that you had gone to medical school instead of doing whatever it is that you ended up doing. You may try to influence your child to become a doctor, and you push so hard that a power struggle results. Power struggles can be dangerous because brilliant children sometimes rebel so hard against parents who try to force them onto a particular career path that they avoid any future plan that is even remotely connected to that path—in this case, science or medicine.

The opposite problem occurs if your child's area of brilliance is something that you just don't understand. You might be a bit shy—someone who always works hard in the background. What if you have a Charmer in your house? How in the world can you begin to conceptualize this phenomenon? You might find yourself viewing your Charmer as a vain attention seeker, but you'll be failing to understand what a terrific area of brilliance this can be if you don't work toward understanding it. You will have to fight the urge to squash your Charmer's amazing ability because of your fears of the problems it could bring with it. You can do this by gathering as much information as you can about the area of brilliance and learning about successful people who live virtuous lives using this area of brilliance for the good of others. (Chapter 11 of this book may be helpful.) Whatever the case, celebrate your child's brilliance, and trust that it is worth pursuing.

Mentors

A mentor is someone, usually not a parent, who shares or intimately understands your child's area of brilliance and can provide a positive example to follow. The mentor can be a teacher, a friend of the family, a relative, a boss, or just someone in the community whom you have sought to assist you in developing your child's area of brilliance. The value of a good mentor cannot be underestimated. Without a mentor, a child may not truly see the value of what she is doing, nor understand how to move forward. You cannot raise your child alone. You need other caring adults to assist you in getting through to her when you cannot, introducing her to opportunities that you may not be familiar with, and acting as a sounding board when you are not sure what to do.

How does a parent find a mentor for a brilliant child? If you are really lucky, mentors will sometimes materialize without much effort. For example, if your child is a Magnet and there is a successful adult Magnet in your extended family, the two will be naturally drawn to each other. Your job will be to explicitly ask the adult Magnet to mentor your child, and then provide opportunities for them to connect and communicate. Mentors in a school or coaching setting also usually happen quite organically and need no specific intervention. You just need to be sure that your child has time in her school day or in or between other activities to connect with this person. In these cases, make a point of thanking the mentor for the extra attention your child is receiving. You might even invite the mentor to your home for a meal or an event. Many times, the mentor becomes a friend of the whole family and finds him- or herself invested in the child's success.

If there is no apparent mentor for your child's area of brilliance, seek one out. Talk with family, friends, neighbors, coworkers, and educators to see if anyone might know someone who could fill this role. You will eventually find someone. Find a way to involve this person in your child's life through lessons or by giving your child a summer job or an internship. Create a structure for the relationship to develop in a healthy, natural way.

Supporters: Friends, Family, School, and Community

A mentor understands what it takes to develop a particular area of brilliance, but your child also needs supporters to keep her on the right track. All children need supporters in their lives—those people who will encourage them and help them move toward their goals. Supporters can be peers or adults from your family, the school, or the community. Help surround your child with supporters.

How can you ensure that people around your child will encourage him to continue on the right path? The first group of supporters you should monitor throughout your child's developmental years are his peers. Be sure that the friends your child surrounds himself with are truly supporters who value his area of brilliance. Likewise, be sure he is a good friend to them and values their areas of brilliance. Help him to understand what areas of brilliance his friends have and how he can help support them. Then be sure that he understands how to recognize when friends are supporting or not supporting his area of brilliance. He should expect them to cheer him on when he pursues his goals, and he should do the same for them. Encourage him to watch their games and performances, and he should ask them to attend his. Your child should think about the things he says to his friends when they announce their accomplishments and expect them to be equally positive toward his.

When I was a teen, I was friends with a group of girls who had very different areas of brilliance. While we didn't always understand each other's pursuits, we were excited for each others' successes, and we helped each other through the tough times and occasional failures. This is what friends do. Be sure your child knows that friends are expected to support each other, even when they don't always understand one another.

You want to ensure that your child has supporters in your immediate and extended families as well. While this starts with you, of course, it also extends to all of the other members of the family. This is particularly important if your child has an area of brilliance that is not easily understood by your relatives. A child who is a Melody Maker among a family of Warriors may seem like a "black sheep." He may be under constant pressure from family members to become more engaged in sports and skip or even drop musical activities. Family members may even ridicule him if they don't understand him. You need to stand up for him if this happens, to make certain that those relatives know what behaviors are acceptable to you when they interact with your child. It is difficult for a child to pursue an area of talent or brilliance if he has little or no support from others.

School and community groups are places where your child will encounter both supporters and detractors. You will have to teach your child how to recognize who is supportive and who is not, and how to deal with difficult situations. If your child attends a school that doesn't seem to value his area of brilliance, he may not feel like he fits in. You may have to assist him in finding a "home" with a caring teacher or within an extracurricular program at the school. The same can be true of community groups. Make sure that any group he joins, whether at your place of worship or through nonprofit organizations or anywhere else, is a place where he will be supported and accepted for who he is. Don't tolerate intolerant people, and teach him to do the same. Talk to him about bullying and how to avoid this destructive behavior, either as a perpetrator or a victim. Most schools and some community organizations have information that can be helpful concerning bullying.[27] Be careful not to tell your child that he just has to learn to fit in. You never want him to compromise who he is and dim his area of brilliance.

Tools and Instruction

Every area of brilliance can be encouraged with the right tools and instruction at the right time. Of course you want to provide your child with everything she needs to become success-ful. However, depending on your child's needs, this can get quite expensive. Additionally, there are plenty of charlatans who prey on families who are trying to assist their children in their pursuits. The most common places you may see this are with vocal instructors, modeling schools, and beauty pageants. While there are certainly reputable groups that provide these types of things, others will exaggerate your child's abilities in order to pry more money out of your pocket. You have to be extremely savvy when parting with cash to help your child pursue her dreams.

Your own child may also play a role in taking your money. Many children become convinced that if they only had that new computer, instrument, costume, or sports gear, they would magi-cally become the next big, famous performer. You need to be dili-gent in evaluating every new tool and instructional opportunity on its own merits. Ask yourself the following questions when making each decision:

- ✔ What do we already have that can do the same thing?

- ✔ What other options are available for a lower cost?

- ✔ What negative consequences will occur if we don't make this purchase?

- ✔ What should I expect my child to contribute to this pur-chase? Can she help pay?

- ✔ Can my child do without something else to contribute to the affordability of this tool, instruction, or experience? What is she willing to give up? (If she is not willing to contribute to the cost, it is probably not worth doing.)

✔ What are the indicators of quality of this tool, instruction, or experience? Is it a program accredited by some authority? Is the person or group providing it a member of a reputable professional organization in the field? Can we talk to anyone else who has used this tool, instruction, or experience for references or advice?

✔ What results should we expect? What good things will happen as a result of purchasing this tool, instruction, or experience?

You will find that if you evaluate the potential purchase using this framework, you will eliminate a great deal of wasted time and money, or even possible damage to your child.

Barriers

There are certainly many barriers to success for your child that can hinder the development of his area of brilliance or even cause it to become derailed. Geography, money (the lack of it), physical health issues, and life events can completely change the course of one's life, often when we least expect it. However, despite these obstacles, you can help your child work through adversity and continue to develop his area of brilliance. Resilience has been shown to be key to success for all children. This trait—the ability to cope with stress and "bounce back" after failure or tragedy—is shared by most people who grow up amidst adversity and yet who still manage to succeed.[28]

Geography

If you live in a community that lacks diversity, and your child does not fit into the cultural norms of that community, he may encounter great barriers to his development. Imagine what it might be like for a male Designer who may be gay and who lives in a rural, fundamentalist Christian community. He may be ridiculed, bullied, and told he is going to Hell on a daily basis. There would likely be tremendous pressure on him to act more masculine and to ditch his Designer ways for more "normal" interests and activities. How can you help this child pursue art and other aspects of his passion that make him feel whole?

What about a female Warrior living in the same community? Or a Melody Maker who lives in a town that has cut music from its only public school? How do you help these children be who they are?

First, make sure that your home is a safe haven for your child. Let her be herself, and provide her with the continual encouragement and acceptance that she may lack in the community. Give her the time, space, and tools in your home that she needs to pursue the development of her area of brilliance. Second, be sure that you stop any harassment or bullying of your child wherever it happens. Talk to adults in the school, and be sure they know that you will not tolerate it. Teach your child how to report bullying to adults and how to respond to it when it happens. Give her the courage to stand up to bullies and not become a victim. If there are other options to a school that has become intolerable to your child, consider them. There may be charter, private, or even homeschool options that will benefit your child.

Third, choose community and religious groups carefully. Be sure that any group you join, or expect your child to join, is tolerant. For example, do not expect your child to attend a place of worship that perpetuates the myth that he is evil. Finally, use technology to your advantage. Thanks to the Internet, children in even the most remote settings can now find solace in groups of people just like them. Help your child connect to a world outside of your small community so he understands that anything is possible.

Don't be afraid of moving to a place where your child may have more access to resources and programs that she needs to nurture her budding exceptional ability. Sometimes this is the best option. Parents of children who are Olympic hopefuls and prodigies in the arts have historically made this choice. The same can be done for children with brilliance in other areas.

Money—The Lack of It

A lack of money is frequently an excuse that parents use to not provide their children with what they need to develop their areas of brilliance. They might think that the instrument costs too much. Or they can't afford to join the swim team. Or there is no money for art supplies. Lack of money can be a barrier, but there are many, many ways to overcome it. The first thing to do is to evaluate how you are spending your money now. Are you paying for unnecessary items that have become routine for you, such as a morning latte or dinner out on Friday nights? Could these things be given up or cut back for a few months or a year? Are there things that you have come to regard as necessities that are really luxuries, like cable television or unlimited texting on your phone? Are there measures you can take to cut your costs? Then, think about ways that you or your child could earn money to provide a particular item or experience for the child.

When my daughter was in high school, my husband became very ill and lost his job. At the same time, I changed jobs and lost a large chunk of my income. Alison is a Melody Maker, and I worried that she would be forever derailed if we stopped voice lessons; still, we really could not afford them. So my daughter and I came up with a solution together. There was a family in our community with five adopted children. This older couple, who became parents of five almost overnight, desperately needed some time away from the kids each week. Alison and I began babysitting every Saturday night for them. This little job paid for her voice lessons and gave us some wonderful time together helping other people. Yes, I was an experienced, highly paid professional, and I took a babysitting gig to help provide for my child's needs. Why not? Most of what our children need is really not all that costly in the greater scheme of things and is often worth the effort it takes to provide it.

Be creative! Sometimes financial assistance is available for certain lessons, camps, or the like. If you are really in dire straits, ask if there is something you can barter in exchange for services for your child, or if there are any scholarships that might help. Talk to the mentors in your child's life to see if they have ideas about financial grants or other assistance. Don't let the lack of money become a barrier in your child's development.

Physical Health

It goes without saying that the most important thing in your child's life is his health. An illness or injury may stop him from developing an area of brilliance. But more often than not, it is our own fears as parents that get in the way of that development. Children are extremely resilient and can usually tell us what they can or cannot do. Be sure that if you are stopping your child from doing something, it is for a legitimate health concern and not because of your own fears.

Children are going to get sick and hurt no matter what we do to prevent it. You have to look at what you can do to mitigate and manage risk, with the understanding that you will never fully eliminate it. If your child happens to be really good at a sport that you consider risky, do all you can to mitigate the risk, listen to medical professionals who advise you, and then let your child keep going if at all possible. If you can't handle watching, then stay home.

If your child is recovering from a severe illness, pursuing the area of brilliance can be the very best medicine of all. It will give him a reason to keep going and to endure what may be a painful recovery. Think of Stephen Hawking and how he has used his incredibly brilliant mind to make advances in science, despite his debilitating illness.[29] Use this as therapy for your child when he needs it. If he is a Warrior and unable to participate in a sport due to injury, help him use the recovery time to read biographies of some favorite athletes. If she is a Melody Maker unable to play her violin for a while, provide her with some marvelous recordings to listen to while she recovers.

Life Events

The worst thing you can do when life hits you hard is to abandon the things you love. Your child's area of brilliance will sustain her when times are tough. Be sure that when her life takes an unexpected turn, she doesn't see it as a barrier to her own development. Instead, help her understand that she can use it to regain her footing in uncharted or seemingly dangerous territory.

Vin Scully, a baseball announcer, has endured some incredible tragedies in his life. Most recently, Scully endured a pair of personal tragedies. He lost his wife from an accidental medical overdose, and his eldest son perished in a helicopter crash. Scully revealed on HBO's *Real Sports with Bryant Gumbel* in July 2005 that his work, in addition to his faith, helped him overcome the grief.

Think about a difficult time in your own life. Did you find yourself getting immersed in work, a hobby, or a cause to get your mind off of things? Getting on with the business of life and seeking out things that give us pleasure help us cope. Children need the same thing.

A Note about Charmers and Magnets

Charmers and Magnets need particular consideration in a discussion on the barriers to developing one's talent or ability. Their areas of brilliance tend to come out in every type of activity. For them, it is not the type of activity that is important; it is the format of the activity and the leadership of it that are the most important considerations. It is easy to confuse these two areas of brilliance—Charmers and Magnets. Charmers are people we feel we have to notice. We want to watch them. Magnets are natural leaders who inspire others to be like them. Charmers are intriguing and fascinating. Magnets are inspiring and compelling.

A Charmer is obvious when she is a model or an actor. It is often not her talent in acting that gains her fame, but rather a luminescent or "star" quality that she possesses. When she joins a sports team, club, or other group, people flock around her. You want to find places where her presence can be an asset to the group. For example, if she volunteers in a facility that assists disadvantaged members of society, she would make a great addition to their fund-raising team. She can be the one who convinces people to part with their money. In a school setting, she is a terrific person to help convince other children to do the right thing or to stir up excitement in a particular group.

A Magnet needs leadership opportunities. He needs to be able to organize and move a group toward a goal. This is quite different from what a Charmer needs, although these two types of children can look very similar. Consider Sarah Palin as an example. She is a Charmer. People are fascinated by her and watch her every move. Yet she quit her job as Governor of Alaska in pursuit of media opportunities. It is my opinion that part of the reason John McCain lost his 2008 bid for presidency with Palin as his running mate was because he was confused by her area of brilliance. She is a Charmer, not a Magnet. A politician needs to be a Magnet in order to get votes and to have a career in this field that is sustainable.

Of course it is possible to be both a Charmer and a Magnet, but you must know which is predominant in your child. Most often she is only one or the other, and you can use your laser focus to point her in the right direction.

It is not enough just to have an area of brilliance. The brilliance must be polished and often focused and clarified. Each special ability and talent must be nurtured in a way that allows the child to grow and develop the gift. Your job as a parent is to help your child focus, like a laser, toward an area of brilliance that will move him toward an exciting and successful life.

CHAPTER 8

The Lens: Reframing Problematic Behaviors in Brilliant Children

Brilliant children sometimes struggle with intensities and sensitivities that can present themselves as behaviors that appear to be problematic and indicative of a behavioral or attention disorder, or even a mental illness. It is important for parents to recognize potential issues and assist their children in overcoming them in order to ensure a successful, healthy future. In fact, good parenting can often prevent behavioral and mental health problems, or at least reduce their severity. Good parenting involves things like developing good communication, advocating for academically challenging schoolwork, establishing routines, setting appropriate limits, and providing nutritious meals and opportunities for exercise.[30] All of these can reduce the risk that your child will develop the kinds of problems that may require medical or psychological help, or even medication. However, despite our best efforts, problems can sometimes occur. Parents may wonder whether they should seek professional help, and that decision can be worrisome.

Sometimes, however, what looks like a problem that many think ought to be treated with medication turns out to be something different. When we frame problematic behaviors in a different light, when we look at the true cause of the problem and not simply at the symptoms, we often see that simple adjustments in the child's environment and routine can solve the issue. It's just a matter of looking at things through a different lens.

When the Solution Is Also the Problem

As you may have heard, in the last several years, there have been huge increases in the amount of medication our children are taking for problems like Attention Deficit Hyperactivity Disorder (ADHD), childhood depression, Obsessive-Compulsive Disorder (OCD), and even Bipolar Disorder. And while these medicines can be a godsend for children with severe problems, they are generally overprescribed and often inappropriate, particularly for brilliant children.[31]

Let's look at what happens when a child is diagnosed with ADHD. The drugs recommended to help alleviate the symptoms of this attention disorder are often prescribed whenever a young person has difficulty sitting still in a classroom. Although more common in boys who demonstrate very high activity levels, girls can also suffer from ADHD, usually exhibited by excessive daydreaming and problems paying attention. Unfortunately, there are no blood tests or other conclusive ways to accurately diagnose ADHD, so doctors rely on behavioral questionnaires submitted by parents and teachers. Questions revolve around the child's ability to complete tasks, engage positively with peers, and sustain attention. The problem with a checklist approach like this is that it assumes that daily tasks being asked of the child are developmentally appropriate and sufficiently engaging for the child's interests and intellectual ability. But if, for example, a seven-year-old boy is required to sit still at his desk reading a textbook that is far below his reading level, it is highly unlikely that he will be able to sustain attention and complete the boring task. A child in this situation can become agitated and emotional about his situation, and he may act out as a result.

Another factor that is not considered on these types of behavioral questionnaires is the existence of structure in the home—including meals, sleep, and home routines. A home with structure, where there are consistent and nutritious family meals, a bedtime routine, appropriate scheduling, limits on screen time, and sufficient attention from parents, can often "cure" the supposed ADHD that seems to be plaguing a child.

Expectations and clear instructions from parents, teachers, and other caregivers are key for brilliant children who seem to suffer from an attention disorder. Take the example of Sanjay. He is eight years old, loves to play computer games and sports, and is an only child. Sanjay's parents have grown worried that he might have ADHD. He is an average student in school, but his teacher reports that he sometimes has difficulty paying attention. At the last parent-teacher conference, the teacher stated that although Sanjay is a very bright child, he is not performing according to his potential. She believes that Sanjay is capable of A's and B's, although he frequently earns C's in her class.

Sanjay's parents, who were in their late 30s when he was born, have worried and perseverated about his every move. After the conference with his teacher, they became extremely concerned that their son would end up being just "average," and they committed to correcting his lackluster performance in school. As soon as they left the school, they called their pediatrician to have Sanjay evaluated. The pediatrician did a basic examination of Sanjay and gave his parents the standard checklist questionnaires. Within a few weeks, Sanjay was on Ritalin and paying more attention in school. And yes, his grades have improved on this controlled medication. He sits still for much longer periods of time and generally completes his homework. His parents report that he is able to follow directions better at home and seems less anxious.

Some people might consider this a success story, but I do not. What I know about Sanjay makes me very concerned that he is medicated with powerful drugs that make life easier for his parents and teachers but that don't really help him live up to his potential. In addition to his "attention" problem, Sanjay has hearing deficit, which came up in routine school testing a year or two before his ADHD diagnosis. Although Sanjay's parents got him the appropriate hearing appliance, he refuses to wear it because he believes other kids will make fun of him. The pediatrician did not even consider that Sanjay's hearing loss could be a factor in his school troubles. I also noticed several other issues in Sanjay's home life that may well contribute to his problem.

First, Sanjay's parents usually fail to provide him with clear, single-step instructions when asking him to complete a task. For example, when they are preparing for school in the mornings, his mother will start by peeking into his room and asking him to get out of bed by saying something like, "Sanjay, do you think you should get up now?" Of course, Sanjay does not think he should do this, so his mother will come back into his room two or three times over the course of about an hour before she finally convinces him to get up. Getting up in the morning is very difficult for Sanjay because he has a tendency to sneak out of bed in the middle of the night to get on the computer or watch television. The poor kid is struggling with severe sleep deprivation.

Once Sanjay is finally roused from slumber, he gets ready for school with the television on in his room. Although his mother pesters him incessantly with general comments about getting ready, the boy frequently forgets what he is supposed to be doing and instead gravitates toward the TV and his favorite morning shows. By the time Sanjay is finally dressed and ready to go to school, there is no time for breakfast, so his mother gives him a sugary toaster pastry to eat in the car on the short drive to school. Once there, they have to wait in the car line for a few minutes before arriving at the entrance, since everyone tends to arrive at the same time. But no worries! Sanjay can pass the time by watching a video in the back seat of the car. By the time they reach the spot where Sanjay can exit the vehicle, the boy has to sprint to class to get there on time.

His teacher reports that he is frequently disheveled and even a bit disoriented when he arrives. He often struggles mightily just to get into the morning routine with the rest of the students.

By mid-morning, following the state-mandated 90 minutes of uninterrupted reading instruction done at his desk, Sanjay is usually a wreck. He hangs off of his chair, doodles, flicks items off of his desk, paces around the classroom, visits the bathroom multiple times, and leaves his assignments only partially completed—hence the teacher's recommendation to talk with the pediatrician.

At 10:30 each morning, the students move to other activities, including math, science, and half-hour "specials" (gym, music, or art). So after 90 minutes of reading activities, requiring him to sit very still, Sanjay goes through three 30-minute periods of instruction in math (usually with some activities involving manipulatives—"teacher-speak" for objects that students can manipulate), science (sometimes with hands-on activities, sometimes not), and gym, music, or art. It usually takes a few minutes for students to travel to each classroom and get organized, so a 30-minute period typically results in about 20 minutes of actual instruction, which may or may not include physical activity, and may or may not be connected to any other learning that goes on in the school day. These periods are challenging for Sanjay because by the time he is able to determine what is expected of him from his several different teachers, which varies virtually every day, it is time to change to the next activity. In addition, teachers of the "special" subjects see up to 150 students every day, so they usually don't know the students as well as the regular classroom teachers do.

Finally, at 12:00, a full three and a half hours after his toaster pastry in the car, Sanjay gets to go to lunch. Lunch is served in a very large, very loud cafeteria, where Sanjay sits in an assigned seat with those children who need extra attention due to their challenging behavior. Sanjay generally eats the school lunch because it is easier for his parents not to have to worry about packing it. These lunches are prepared according to national school lunch standards, and a typical meal might include a grilled cheese sandwich, tater tots, corn, and pudding. Most school lunch menus contain almost all processed foods, much of which is deep fried and laden with fat and sodium and is high in carbohydrates, include very little in the way of fresh fruits and vegetables, and are fairly low in protein.

At 12:30, Sanjay is free to roam the playground for 15 minutes. There are typically about 125 children out at the same time, with a couple of teachers supervising them. The big game at Sanjay's school is usually kickball, which the students initiate and organize themselves. Since there are so many children who want to play, it takes a few minutes for them to pick their teams. Because Sanjay is somewhat small and not known for his athletic prowess, he is generally not among the first picked. As he waits for a team captain to call his name, he becomes agitated. All he wants to do is play, and he has to wait and wait. While he waits, he kicks the dirt and, in doing so, accidentally kicks the girl next to him. She begins screaming, and one of the teachers comes to her aid. When the teacher learns that Sanjay kicked her, she directs him to sit on a bench for the duration of recess.

At 12:45, Sanjay returns to his classroom to continue the math lesson that was started earlier in the day. He is required to find the materials that he was using then and pick up where he left off, working with two other students. This is a challenge for him. He cannot remember what the instructions were and has lost some of the things he needs to complete the lesson. He begins searching in his desk for some missing cut-out paper shapes while the other two children in his group move on without him. Unable to locate his materials, Sanjay's attention shifts to a paper fortune-teller toy that he made the previous week. He starts to play with it and, in the process, spills most of the contents of his desk. The teacher, becoming more and more frustrated with Sanjay, sends him to a "time out" desk in the back of the classroom, where he is told to read quietly while the other students complete the math task.

At about 2:00, Sanjay is allowed to rejoin his group and is able to keep it together for the remainder of the day. However, his body needs to move, so when the class is dismissed for the day, he bolts passed the other children and tries to reach the student pick-up area as quickly as possible. In the process, he spills some of the contents of his backpack, which he has failed to adequately zip, and he doesn't retrieve everything before getting into his father's car, which is awaiting him in the car line.

By the time Sanjay and his father arrive home, Sanjay realizes that he has lost the worksheet he needs to do for homework, and an argument ensues with his parents over his lack of responsibility. Eventually, Sanjay and his parents eat dinner, although not at the same time, and Sanjay retreats to his bedroom, where he can play computer games and watch television by himself until his parents start pestering him to clean up and get ready for bed.

This cycle of activity goes on in many American households every day. But imagine if Sanjay's life was structured a little differently....

Sanjay wakes up in the morning to an alarm clock that his mother has taught him to set himself. He has no trouble getting up on time because he went to bed a full nine hours earlier, after a dinner with his parents, an evening bath, and 30 minutes of reading on the couch next to his father. They have been reading *The Hobbit* together for the past couple of weeks, and Sanjay cannot wait to hear what happens next.

Right after Sanjay gets up, his mother gives him clear, individual instructions for each task that she wants him to complete. She tells him to come into the kitchen first and eat breakfast. She ensures that he has wholesome food (not processed) with high protein, whole grains, and a moderate amount of fat. These are the kinds of foods that give the brain enough fuel for the day. Then she tells him to go into the bathroom to wash his hands and brush his teeth. Once that is done, she directs him to put on this clothes, which he has selected the night before and laid on the chair in his bedroom. Once he is dressed, she tells Sanjay to brush his hair. She also makes sure he is wearing his hearing aids. Finally, she reminds him to pick up his dirty PJs and make his bed. She gets his lunch together and puts it next to his backpack. Together they grab their bags that are already waiting by the front door and which contain everything they need for the day.

Sanjay and his mother begin walking toward the school. At the corner, he meets up with several friends and another parent who is waiting to walk the group the short distance to the school. His mother waves good-bye to him, walks back to the house, and gets into her car to go to work. Sanjay enjoys the time to stretch his legs, breathe the fresh air, and talk with his friends on the way to school. He arrives in plenty of time, without stress, to unpack his backpack and get ready for the start of the school day.

Imagine that kind of structure in a child's home life, and now imagine if the school day were just a bit different. Instead of a state-mandated 90-minute reading block to begin the day, suppose the students started with some type of activity designed to get the brain moving and synchronizing. Sanjay might enjoy the violin, or even a hip-hop dance class. After 30 minutes, the students settle into reading activities of their choice. The classroom and common area just outside of the room include comfy pillows and chairs so that the students can relax while they read and participate in book circles. The teacher pulls small groups of students during this time to work on targeted skills according to their individual reading needs. After about an hour, the students enjoy snacks they have brought with them or that are provided by the school. This is usually fruit and/ or nuts. The teacher also ensures that the students all drink some water so they are well hydrated.

At about 10:45, students move into math activities for an hour. These are handled in a similar fashion to reading. There are a variety of activities to engage the students, who can spread out into various comfortable spots. The teacher pulls small groups of students to work on targeted instruction. Other students have a menu of options geared toward their individual learning needs. Some work on games with manipulatives, some work on the computers, while others help each other on the white board. At 11:45, students regroup and enjoy a short activity designed to prepare them to transition to lunch. This might involve the teacher reading aloud to them, or group practice of multiplication facts, or perhaps a game that the teacher has previously taught the class.

At noon, the students go to lunch—but they do not go into the large cafeteria space. Instead, they eat in groups about one quarter of this size, where they enjoy family-style meals or the lunches they have brought from home. This time, the school lunch menu includes fruits and veggies from a local farming cooperative, as well as other non-processed foods. Great care is taken to ensure that students get a good, healthy meal. Sanjay has brought his lunch from home, which includes a trail mix, some cheese, an apple, and celery sticks with peanut butter. He also finishes off the bottle of water he brought with him in the morning.

After lunch, the students go outside for 30 minutes of recess. But unlike in our last example, there are more teachers available to supervise and assist the students in engaging in some type of activity. The goal is for students to manage their own fun, but the teachers help by setting up stations where they can go and get right into the action. To facilitate this, the school uses a group of older students who are also peer mediators to help the younger ones learn playground games. One group does a walk/jog around the field. In the corner nearest the school building, children are playing hopscotch and jump rope. In the center of the playground, there is a kickball game led by sixth graders. The older students make sure that the game starts immediately by quickly counting off students and putting them into teams in which everyone gets a turn. There is also a group of children who are building things with blocks and other objects that they have found among the trees. Of course there are occasional conflicts, but most of the time, students enjoy recess and use this time to build friendships, develop social skills, imagine, play, and move.

After a half hour of fresh air and sunshine, the students are ready to get back to work. The afternoon includes those "specials" of either gym, music, or art. Each class gets something different from what they did in the morning, so if Sanjay's group began the day with violin, they do either art or gym in the afternoon. However, this period is longer (about 45 minutes), and the students have the same "special" for a week at a time. This gives the teacher the ability to plan a full unit for each group of students that can be rotated. The students don't have to make as many transitions with this type of scheduling, and it can be integrated with the learning that is taking place in the academic classes. Social studies and science projects round out the rest of the school day, along with some time to prepare for the transition home in the afternoon.

The teacher reserves about 20 minutes at the end of the day for students to get ready to go. Each student has a buddy. They check each other's backpacks to ensure that they have everything they need, and they assist each other in zipping up and getting ready to walk out of the classroom on time. Sanjay is excited to see his dad as he approaches the pick-up area. It is his turn to walk the group of neighborhood children home in the afternoon.

When they arrive home, Sanjay and his father go inside the house and enjoy a snack together as they review the boy's folder and notes for the day. Sanjay's dad assists him in getting his homework done by monitoring his progress and giving him individual instructions for each task if he needs it. After homework is complete, Sanjay is allowed to go outside and play with his neighborhood friends while his father finishes up sending a few emails and completing work tasks. After his mother comes home, they sit down to dinner as a family before enjoying a little TV together. At the end of a fun, productive day, Sanjay reads with his father, takes a bath, and goes to bed early enough so that he can get nine hours of sleep. He does not have a TV or a computer in his bedroom, so there is no chance for him to sneak in these activities in the middle of the night.

How do you think Sanjay's behavior might be different with the second scenario? Although I have met a few children in my quarter-century as an educator who really needed serious medication for attention issues, almost all of my students were able to function beautifully if they were provided with a structure similar to the one described here. You may be thinking, "But this is idealistic and cannot be replicated in places where kids spend long hours in after-school care, or where they can't walk to and from school." While it is true that we may not be able to employ all of these strategies, most parents and teachers can do most of them. It just takes commitment to focusing on what our children need, and not bowing to pressures to make things more convenient. Children deserve to have good food and enough rest. They deserve time to be with their parents without distraction, as well as time to be with other children on a playground. If we want our children to grow into well-balanced, healthy adults, we need to create an environment that honors their development and where they can be well-balanced, healthy kids.

Is It Just the Environment, or Is There a Bigger Issue?

So how do you know if your child is the rare one who really *does* need medical intervention, whether for ADHD, depression, learning to manage anger, fearfulness, or problems getting along with others? First, do the things described in this chapter. The good news is that even if your child needs medication, these suggestions will still help. After you are sure that you have covered all of the bases—nutrition, rest, and developmentally appropriate and balanced activities—you should notice better, more focused behavior from your child. If things don't improve significantly after a few weeks, though, you may want to start exploring the possibilities of medical intervention.

Your most important consideration should be whether or not your child is suffering. If she is truly suffering, consider seeking help. If she is frequently distraught, angry, or sad, she is telling you that something is wrong. Watch for temper tantrums when she is the middle of tasks, disorientation, or a complete lack of friendships (not even one). Talk to her, and listen for the following types of statements:

> ✔ "Sometimes I see the stuff happening around me, and I feel like I'm watching a movie. I can't really be part of it; I just watch everyone else."

✔ "I feel like I can never finish anything. I get mad when it isn't right, and I just do something else."

✔ "I don't have any friends. There is nobody I want to play with."

✔ "I don't belong here. I don't really want to be part of this world."

✔ "I think the world would be better off without me."

If your child exhibits any of these symptoms or makes statements similar to the ones listed here, *despite the changes you have already made*, it may be time to consult with a psychologist or a physician.

Selecting a Doctor

Selecting a physician is probably the most important decision you can make to address your child's behavioral and mental health. Although pediatricians are experts at what developmental milestones should be and will generally prescribe medication for ADHD or depression, they may not be the best people to work with if you think your child may be suffering from an attention disorder or a mental health problem. Try to find a pediatric neurologist or a psychologist or psychiatrist who specializes in childhood mental health and who also has some knowledge about common issues for children with advanced abilities.[32] This person should be up to date on the latest types of assessments that go way beyond the guesswork associated with simple questionnaires. In addition, this doctor should screen your child for any autoimmune diseases, parasites, or other problems that might mimic the symptoms of mental health disorders. He or she should also be able to establish a good rapport with your child and form a partnership with you to improve your child's life.

The Stigma

Mental illness still carries a stigma in our country, and it can be challenging to locate and secure appropriate care and treatment for a child who is diagnosed with one of many possible conditions. As a parent, please remember the following:

- ✔ Mental illness can occur in any child, regardless of his or her area of brilliance.

- ✔ The earlier you diagnose mental illness, the greater your child's chances of overcoming it are.

- ✔ Do *not* rely on your pediatrician to diagnose, treat, or manage mental illness. Seek out professionals with specific expertise who can best guide you.

- ✔ Remember that children are often misdiagnosed. Many children with severe mental illness are immediately labeled as ADHD and put on medicines that can exacerbate their problems. Beware of quick diagnoses that rely solely on behavioral checklists or questionnaires.

- ✔ Some autoimmune conditions or parasites can mimic mental illness, so be sure to rule out other causes of symptoms.

Brilliant children can have mental health issues just like other children. It is critical that you stay on guard to treat these if they present themselves, but not medicate problems that are mere symptoms of a life that is out of balance.

CHAPTER 9

Striking the Match:
Motivating Your Brilliant Child

Strike a match too gently, and you won't even get a spark. Strike it too hard, and you may get a spark but no flame. In order to ignite a fire, you must strike the match with just the right amount of pressure and friction.

Creating motivation in a brilliant child is like that. Encourage too gently, and the child may not move toward her passions. Push too hard, and she will turn or cease to move all together. Your brilliant child needs drive in order to truly develop her gifts. You will need to help her develop the drive that will make her want to do things, to be somebody.

We live in a time and place when motivation—at least the kind that comes from inside a person—can sometimes be in short supply for our children.[33] The "millennial" generation is coming of age at a time when we have more resources and material goods than ever before in the history of the world. Even in the context of our economic downturn, most people have maintained an extraordinarily high standard of living, in which nearly every child has a cell phone, a computer, plenty of clothes and toys, multiple electronic devices, and maybe even a car.[34]

Most American children want for little. In addition, with our society's increasing emphasis on making sure that no one's feelings are hurt, many children today are rewarded as "winners" even when they have accomplished nothing. But in order for our children to become self-motivated to achieve, parents must create an environment where their children do want for things and feel encouraged to move toward independence and success.

Brilliant children usually have to exert little effort to achieve in school. In fact, some experts argue that by not providing them with enough challenging work, we are actually teaching our bright children to underachieve.[35] However, when we allow our children to do this, we are handicapping them by denying them the opportunity to learn important life skills like diligence, resilience, and frustration tolerance. Children who coast through school often find that they don't know how to handle challenges when they do arise. We want them to encounter challenges so they can learn how to manage frustrating situations and become self-managing, self-reliant, independent, competitive individuals.

Become a Pathfinder Parent

The first step in the process of helping to motivate your brilliant child is for you to become a "pathfinder" parent. Like a pathfinder in the military, the pathfinder parent checks out the conditions and potential dangers that lie ahead for the child and provides the guidance that the child needs to deal with whatever obstacles occur. This is in stark contrast to the "helicopter" or the "hot air balloon" parenting styles that are so common today. A helicopter parent, as the name implies, hovers over the child, protecting him from challenge and difficulty, ensuring that his life is always trouble free, comfortable, and easy. She solves her child's problems for him whenever possible. A hot air balloon parent does not believe that she can influence her child to any degree and chooses not to interfere, even when the child is making important decisions. She ignores her child's problems. There clearly needs to be an alternative approach, which I believe is the pathfinder parent, who determines her level of intervention based on the child's temperament and the type of issue at hand. Her goal is to teach her child to manage and solve his own problems.

If you want to be a pathfinder parent, take the time to evaluate each situation and determine what level of intervention makes sense. Always give your child as much independence as possible in the decision-making process, yet do not allow him to do things that will truly endanger his life, health, or future. Here is a framework that may help you in your decision making as a pathfinder parent.

There are three different types of issues that require three different types of interventions: red light, yellow light, and green light. A red light problem is so serious that it has life-threatening or life-altering consequences. When faced with a red light issue, a pathfinder parent will step in and make decisions for the child, ensuring that he doesn't do anything that will cause irreparable harm. Examples of red light issues are drug use, an abusive relationship, or dropping out of high school. Pathfinder parents do not allow children to make choices in these situations. They immediately take control and try to help the child understand why.

Yellow light issues are problems that might cause some difficulty, moderate levels of inconvenience or consequences, or loss of modest amounts of money. Examples of yellow light issues are losing a cell phone, taking a school course that is not the best choice, failing to pay a traffic ticket on time, or perhaps even being bullied. A pathfinder parent will assist the child in considering alternatives and determining the best choices but will still allow the child to make the decisions.

Finally, green light issues are choices that result in mild inconvenience or consequences, poor grades, or the loss of a little bit of money. These might include forgetting homework, arguing with friends, or spending allowance money unwisely on items that the child doesn't really need. Pathfinder parents will not intervene in these instances, allowing the child to experience natural consequences fully, and then assist the child in processing what happened afterward.

Remove the Plastic Bubble

Think about the process of learning to walk. Before your child takes her first steps on her own, you hold her hands to steady her. She then begins cruising the furniture and tentatively ventures a step or two beyond before falling down. As she gains competence and confidence, you allow her to take more steps on her own in a greater variety of locations. Before you know it, she is walking around the house and eventually running down the street. What would happen if you never let go of her hands?

In many respects, some parents today attempt to keep their children in a plastic bubble, free from all potential harm. These parents are afraid to allow their children to play outside or walk to school because they fear predators may be lurking. They may prevent their kids from engaging in activities like skateboarding or diving, fearing certain death. As soon as the child feels emotional distress, they may allow her to quit activities like performing in a school play or entering an athletic competition. Now I am not suggesting that you allow your child to be in danger, but it is important that you maintain a correct sense of risk, mitigate the risk as much as possible, and then allow your child to live a full life.

Think about stranger danger. Although many people believe that the world today is a dangerous place, violent crime in the United States has actually decreased during the last 40 years.[36] Teens and young adults, who experience the highest rates of violent crime, are now less likely to become victims than ever before.[37] There are only 115 cases of stranger abduction across the U.S. annually, according to the U.S. Department of Justice.[38] Although each case is horrendous and tragic, and there are 115 too many, this is hardly an epidemic. Yet there are plenty of parents who will not allow their children outside without immediate supervision by an adult for fear that their child will be abducted.

So what is a parent to do? Mitigate the risk by setting boundaries or limits for your child's outdoor play, as well as establishing safe routes for walking to and from school, and then allow freedom within those boundaries. Make sure your child is always with a group. Teach him how to stay safe by walking quickly away from cars that are slowing down near him and ignoring strangers who try to lure him with candy, gifts, puppies, or pleas for help. If appropriate, have your child carry a cell phone. Teaching him how to evaluate situations and to stay safe is much more effective at preparing him for a bright future than locking him inside the house until adulthood.

Ironically, statistics show us that children are more in danger indoors than outside, thanks to the Internet. One out of every 25 youngsters is solicited sexually online, and this includes attempts to contact the children offline, which often result in actual victimizations. Keep in mind, however, that about one-fourth of these solicitations come from people the children actually know, and in most cases, they're other youngsters.[39]

Monitor your child's use of the computer. If you must, password protect your Internet access so that he can only get online when you are present and can enter the password, or purchase software that allows you to track what websites have been visited—and tell your child that you have the ability to do this. Help him to understand the dangers of connecting with people online whom he doesn't know. The Internet is a wonderful tool that can help us learn amazing new things with the click of a mouse, and we want our children to have access to this information. However, children have to learn to use the Internet and social networking safely.

Make sure that your child has opportunities to challenge herself emotionally and physically. You want her to be able to ride a bike, learn to skateboard, or ride a scooter. Teach her the rules of the road, show her potential hazards, and ensure that she wears a helmet *every* time. You want her to safely endure experiences that might feel difficult to her, like appearing on a stage or singing in public. If she gets scared and wants to quit, talk about her fears, and help her get beyond them. This will build her self-esteem in a way that nothing else can. After all, self-esteem is not developed by doing easy tasks; it evolves as we master tasks that are progressively more challenging and difficult.

Decrease Rewards

In our efforts to improve a child's behavior, we sometimes offer tangible rewards when they are not necessary, and yet this may actually hinder the child's motivation to learn and achieve. Extrinsic rewards such as stickers or trinkets can *decrease* the likelihood that your child will seek to master new challenges. Studies on motivation that have been replicated around the world are very clear on this issue. And if a task requires thinking and logic, rather than a simple behavior change, your child will be even less motivated by tangible rewards like money or a cell phone. So if you are offering your child money for good grades, you may be increasing the chances that his grades will go down. You are also increasing the likelihood that he may become addicted to external rewards. A better approach to developing self-motivation is to encourage him by recognizing and praising effort and its relationship to the end result.[40]

Allow Natural Consequences

Parents who allow natural consequences to occur are much more likely to help their children change their behavior. One area where parents particularly tend to jump to their children's rescue is bringing required items to school. As a principal, I watched some moms make up to three trips to the school in a single day because their children forgot things. When I asked why, they invariably told me just how distressed their kids were, and they didn't want them to get a bad grade or eat a lunch they didn't like or be excluded from something, etc., etc. The children who were lucky enough to have parents who simply could not run to school every time they forgot something learned to forget less often and worked harder at being prepared each day. Children need to feel distress occasionally if they are to learn the lessons of responsibility.

Children, no matter how bright, should be required to participate in completing some of the household chores. If those chores specifically benefit them, they will learn the importance of doing them, as well as what happens when they don't do them. As an example, have your child do her own laundry. She will become more responsible if she wants to be able to wear her favorite jeans and has to rely on herself to wash them. Kids can start doing their own laundry at a very young age, which has the added benefit of lessening the work load for parents.

There are plenty of ways in which parents can allow their children to learn the natural consequences of their actions. Anything that is a green light issue, as well as some yellow light issues, can help children learn how to become responsible for their actions. It is only by learning from our mistakes that we discover resilience and independence.

Reduce Comfort

In this age of affluence in America, we have gotten pretty comfortable, and our children are even more so. We have climate-controlled indoor spaces, so we never have to be hot or cold. Our televisions, sound systems, garage doors, and many other gadgets are controlled with remotes so that we can be in complete command without lifting more than a finger to press the buttons. We have food whenever we want it, we carry phones and the Internet right in our pockets, we have multiple cars in our garages so that everyone can get where they want to go, and there are all kinds of entertainment in nearly every room in the house.

But making things easy isn't a good way to motivate our brilliant children to achieve. If we want our children to have that "fire in the belly" to work hard and accomplish things they can be proud of, we have to reduce their comfort. I am not, of course, talking about depriving children to the point of abuse, but rather of simply not providing luxuries that are not needed. This should ideally start at a very young age.

Consider diapers and strollers. Potty training is occurring at older ages than in previous generations. The main motivation for a child to want to become toilet trained used to be discomfort. Once the baby notices the discomfort of a wet diaper, she is motivated to learn how to use the potty to avoid it. However, thanks to the convenience of highly absorbent diapers and pull-ups that feel dry to the child, this is no longer an issue, and young children are content to remain in diapers indefinitely. The result is a generation of children who aren't potty trained until the average age of over two years, as compared to 18 months in the 1950s.[41]

When our daughter was about 20 months old, she got a diaper rash that became infected. This was when diapers first started including the gel that allows them to be extremely absorbent but also very thin. It turned out that Alison was allergic to the gel, so the doctor advised changing to cloth diapers. Within just a few days, our daughter decided that she no longer wanted to wear diapers and began using the potty. We never had to do a thing, and she really never had any accidents. If you want to accelerate potty training, change to cloth diapers or some of the newer disposable models that allow your child to feel the wetness.

Strollers have also become much more comfortable—for children and for the adults who push them. They are bigger and more plush than ever before, and they are equipped with cup holders, toys, and lots of gadgets to make travel more convenient. When children are about two, they *should* start to want to walk on their own, but parents let them extend their time in the strollers because they are comfortable. Additionally, it is much more convenient for parents to restrain children in a stroller so they can shop and walk rather than worry about having a little one to supervise.

If the strollers were still the smaller, more rigid styles, children would not want to stay in them; those types weren't comfortable. But now, in the soft, larger seats, with room and attachments for drinks, food, and toys, children just sit back and relax. If you want your child to desire abandoning the stroller, try switching to an inexpensive, small, folding model. He may jump up and out in no time! This will require you to take on a much more active role in guarding his safety when you are out and about, but the benefit will be a child who becomes more independent as he grows.

There are lots of opportunities for turning discomfort into motivation. If your car is equipped with video players for your children, disconnect the videos and hand your children books or old-fashioned car games. Don't let them be passively entertained, but rather actively engaged and interested in what they are doing. You can also use time in the car for communicating with one another.

If you have a preteen or teen who doesn't want to connect with the family and hibernates in her room, remove the things there that make it a comfortable place to be, like television, computers, and phones. Don't give your children their own everything. Insist that they share the television or computer with others in the house. As your child grows up, discomfort is one of the keys to encouraging her to get out on her own. Keep the creature comforts to a minimum, and require her to pitch in with chores and finances so that she will be more prepared to live on her own later. This includes adult children who move back in with their own children. Limit their space in your home so that they will want to spread out in a place of their own. When your child becomes old enough to drive, be sure she gets her license. Stop chauffeuring her everywhere she wants to go so that she will have a desire to transport herself.[42]

Delay Gratification

Work ethic is created when a child learns to delay gratification for greater good in the long term. Simply put, kids who learn to wait for things that are important will work hard to make them happen. This tendency can and should be taught at an early age. Of course, this is easier said than done in a culture that has instant everything.

When I was growing up, we were allowed to ride our bikes to the 7-11 store every Saturday and use a portion of our allowance to buy a Slurpee. I started doing this with my older sisters when I was only about six years old. I remember saving my coins so that I would have enough each week to get the size and flavor that I wanted. This became a special event because it only happened on Saturdays when the weather was good. I learned to wait, save money, and deal with disappointment if the weather was bad and I had to wait until the following week. Likewise, birthdays and Christmas were important to us because they were the only times that our parents bought us toys. We had plenty, like most kids growing up in the 1960s and '70s, but we didn't get a toy with every fast-food meal, and we only got really special items on special occasions.

Many children today are accustomed to getting what they want when they want it. And with the advent of video and the Internet, they can watch special programs over and over whenever they want and have access to unlimited games, music, and multimedia. Unfortunately, some parents today seem to equate their value in their children's eyes with the amount of material goods they provide them.

Certainly, we can't simply think that returning to bygone days is the answer. There is much more abundance in our culture today, and our children are living in the midst of it. So instead, think about how you can encourage your children to save and plan for the future in our "I-want-it-now" world. Carefully consider when and how much you get for your children. Think about limiting access to certain media to make it special. For example, if you want your children to enjoy the holiday television specials, put them away for most of the year, and only show them in December. If you buy fast-food meals with toys, limit the number your child can have at any given time, and donate the rest. Or buy a sandwich without the toy, allowing it only at certain times.

Provide a real budget for your child beginning in about fifth or sixth grade. Teach him how to manage his money by providing him with a monthly allowance. Consider all of the money you normally spend on him each month, including school lunches, school trips, clothes (take your annual average amount and divide by 12), and maybe one special event, like going to the movies. Give him all of the money at the beginning of the month. You can set up a special account for this purpose with a debit card, or use cash. Work with him to establish a budget, and discuss ways to save money, like packing his own lunch. Then find one item that he might want to buy in the future, like a popular electronic gadget. Help him determine how much he can spend and how much he would like to save so that he can get that item.

Now, here is the hard part. Do *not* bail him out when he over-spends (and he probably will, at least initially). If he blows all of his money at the beginning of the month on a couple of video games that he just *has* to have, he will be packing his lunch for the rest of the month and will have to say no to his friends who invite him to the movies. After just a few of these types of incidents, he will be on the road to budgeting his money and financial success.

The most important lesson to teach your child about money, particularly if you are well off, is that he has nothing. A child does not really own anything. With the exception of rare child profes-sional performers or athletes, a child cannot legally own anything. Be sure your child knows that even if you make a lot of money, he is actually poor. If he wants to earn his own money, you can help him do that, but even the very best babysitter and minimum wage earner is still pretty poor.

You might want to talk to your child about how much money you make and involve him in your own budgeting process so he can gain a real understanding of the value of the dollar. Tell him about times when money was tighter. If you are in the unfortunate situation of being in dire financial straits, talk about that as well. Discuss events that have happened that have caused your problem so that he might learn from them. If you have made mistakes, be open about them, and help him understand them. If you are the victim of circumstances, discuss some ways that he might set him-self up to avoid similar situations. Talk together about what you can do as a family to ease the financial burden. Children want to be part of the solutions to problems, and bright children are able to understand priorities and budgeting at a fairly young age. They can help by finding discount coupons, collecting recyclables, turning off power strips and lights, and making do with less.

Encourage Accomplishment

Self-esteem is created by accomplishment; accomplishment does not occur simply as a result of self-esteem. But somehow, many parents and educators today have confused the research, thinking that the more we praise our children, the more they will accomplish. Children feel good about themselves as a result of succeeding in doing things they find interesting, relevant, and challenging. Research[43] reveals that praising sustained effort motivates children, while praising innate ability does not. Further research on accomplishment reveals that expertise in an area requires about 10 years or 10,000 hours of time spent working in the area.[44] This research suggests that although innate ability plays a role, sustained practice over time can be at least as important, allowing children to develop their talents. So our job as parents in this area requires that we provide challenges and then reward sustained effort and true accomplishment resulting from that effort.

Think of all of the practices in our culture that are completely contrary to this notion. We award diplomas to four-year-olds wearing caps and gowns at preschool commencement ceremonies. We have sports leagues in which everyone gets a trophy just for participating. We reduce competition as much as possible because we don't want our little ones to experience losing. There are educators and even entire school districts that don't like the idea of gifted programs because they might make the rest of the students feel inadequate. Some schools no longer have valedictorians because it might make the other children feel bad.

You *can* buck these trends. Don't allow your preschooler to participate in graduation events. Don't accept participation trophies. If you are the parent in charge of organizing these types of events, structure them to reward true effort and accomplishment. Think about the messages you are sending with each ritual and celebration.

Allow your child to lose at games with you, and provide increasing levels of competition as she grows older. Above all, expect a lot from your child. Give her honest feedback about her sustained effort, as well as the results of that effort. If you think she can do better, tell her exactly what she needs to do to make it happen. She will almost always rise to the occasion. Keep in mind, though, that different children have different temperaments. You will need to be careful that your child doesn't internalize your honest feedback as the belief that she must always be perfect. The encouragement should focus on the striving, not on the outcome. In this way, think of yourself more like a coach, guiding your child toward adulthood.

Control the Crowd

Your child's motivation is likely to be affected by the motivation levels of his peers. Discuss what you expect to see in the friends your child chooses. Tell him that you like seeing him with other kids who are involved in healthy activities and clubs and who work hard. Be sure that you talk to his friends to see for yourself just how driven they are. We are only as good as the people who surround us. Require that your child surround himself with good, driven, successful people.

Create a Sense of Purpose

The work that we adults do to make money may or may not provide us with a sense of purpose. Think about yourself and other adults in your life. What does each person do to create meaning in his or her life? Those who are very lucky have jobs that pay them to fulfill their sense of purpose. But many others do something outside of a paying job that is their passion. This might be sailing, or running a program for homeless people, or leading religious instruction, or playing golf, or performing in the local community theater. Children are no different. We want them to develop passions in life. These are the things that will make them jump out of bed in the morning, eager to embrace the day.

As parents, we sometimes derail our children's sense of passion with our own anxieties about how they will someday earn a living. So many parents indulge their children's interest in performing arts through middle school, only to stop supporting these things as the children enter high school. Once their children begin high school, these same parents tell their children how they must now "get serious" and focus on courses and programs that will get them into college.

The truth is that much of what children learn from the arts is the very stuff that will make them more successful in college. But in our standards-driven educational system, it is easy to lose sight of that. In reality, anything that is relevant to a child is important, and we should do all we can to fuel her passions and encourage her to explore all of the possibilities that life has to offer. The National Association for Gifted Children has recognized the important role that motivation plays in the development of abilities. Its latest definition[45] speaks to "high levels of motivation" in a particular domain and acknowledges that "The development of ability or talent is a lifelong process."

The most important aspect of parenting a brilliant child is recognizing what motivates that child. You want to develop his passions while keeping all of the other factors described in this chapter in balance. If you have a Warrior, and your two competitive leagues keep your 12-year-old (and you) on the road five days a week, you may want to consider dropping one league and helping your child explore other areas that might also be exciting.

Sometimes parents push too hard in a child's area of brilliance, and sometimes they don't push enough. Either of these tendencies can cause brilliant children to lose motivation and the power to propel their lives forward.[46] Keep children motivated by allowing them to step out of their comfort zones and risk the natural consequences of making their own way in life. Only by doing these types of things can our children truly become independent and self-directed learners.

We are the parents, and in many ways, we know what's better for our children than they do. We don't want our kids simply seeking to conform and fit in so that they are passively entertained in a society of conspicuous consumption of material goods, and it is up to us as parents to give direction and to actively set boundaries and limits. On the other hand, it would not be appropriate for us to simply live out our life dreams through the achievements of our children. We don't want them to achieve only in areas that we select.

We want them to be high achievers, but along pathways that they select with our guidance.

Our children—brilliant children in particular—need challenge in their lives. They need to be motivated to achieve all that they are capable of achieving. This is not always easy, but we need to teach them that they do not have to conform to peer pressure; they do not have to have every convenience and electronic gadget that their friends have. In fact, creative adults tend to have had child-hoods replete with deprivation of some sort.[47] Of course, I am not recommending major deprivation of any kind, but our children should be exposed to various kinds of challenge. This promotes self-management and independence—qualities which will serve our brilliant children well in adulthood.

CHAPTER 10

Fanning the Flame: Preparing Your Child for a Brilliant Future

Allison Hooper majored in French in college and decided to study abroad in France for a semester. When the semester ended, she did not want to go home. So she wrote to farmers around the countryside to see if she could work on a farm in exchange for room and board for the summer. A farm in Brittany offered her a position and allowed her to continue her immersion in the French culture that she loved so much. This farm made artisan cheese, and Allison was able to learn this craft, virtually unknown in the United States.

After completing her degree in French and working on other farms in Europe, Allison eventually returned to the United States, pursued continuing education in agriculture, and worked as a lab technician (no French required) for the Vermont Department of Agriculture. Bob Reese, marketing director for the agency, asked Allison for assistance when he was preparing a state dinner requiring cheese. From that partnership, the Vermont Butter and Cheese Company was born. In addition to running this multi-million dollar business with Bob, Allison has had a book about cheese published and has become an artisan cheese and butter evangelist for America.

What would have happened to Allison if she had parents who discouraged her love for the French language or who insisted that she have a distinct plan for her post-college years? Nobody could have predicted that Allison would go to France and fall in love with cheese, allowing her to launch a highly successful business and pioneer the making of European style dairy products in the United States.

The truth is that there are only a handful of careers that have a clear path and a distinct major in college. Most of us will have several careers in our lifetime, and many different jobs. Yet each experience provides us with skills or knowledge that we take to the next, eventually finding where we should be. The best gift we can give our children is the permission to follow their passions. While they are in middle and high school, we can provide them with as many experiences as possible and try to fan the flames of interest they get along the way. Then, we need to sit back, relax, and enjoy the ride.

Educational Value

The two top definitions for the word "education" from www. dictionary.com reveal the challenge that many parents experience in guiding their children's formal schooling:

Education:

the act or process of imparting or acquiring general knowledge, developing the powers of reasoning and judgment, and generally of preparing oneself or others intellectually for mature life

the act or process of imparting or acquiring particular knowledge or skills, as for a profession

The first definition focuses on preparation for life, while the second stresses the preparation for a particular profession. Lisa

Rivero, in *A Parent's Guide to Gifted Teens*, distinguishes between "parenting for college" and "parenting for life." Have you thought about your mission as a parent and how this might influence the educational plans you are mapping out for your child?

While it is certainly appropriate for a college student to major in engineering, or teaching, or nursing, or another specific profession, this is not necessarily the best idea. Most children are unsure of what they want to do as adults, and yet they are pressured by teachers, parents, guidance counselors, and others to have a specific plan for their life's work. Not only is this difficult for young people to do—especially if they have more than one area of passion—it is nearly impossible to forecast what careers will even be available in the future. Many of the jobs that exist today were not even thought of a decade ago. With the acceleration of information and technology, we cannot know the vast opportunities that will exist in the next five, 10, or 20 years. So instead of pushing your child to identify a career path and a college major to match, assist her in finding her passion and moving toward that.

Newton's First Law

Isaac Newton's first law of motion explains that things at rest remain at rest until a force is acted upon them, and things that are in motion stay in motion unless something exerts pressure on them to stop. This is important to remember as your child grows older and moves toward adulthood. You want him to be moving, exploring, creating, learning, and discovering. His career will develop as a result of that movement. Meanwhile, if you have done a good job instilling drive by reducing comfort and rewards, teaching him to delay gratification, and building self-esteem through accomplishment, he will find ways to feed and clothe himself. If you have also ensured that he surrounds himself with good friends who are equally driven, he will be continually encouraged, and the acceleration of his motion will increase.

Keep the following points in mind if you become concerned about your child's career or educational choices:

✔ Does he show enthusiasm about things he is learning and experiencing?

✔ Is he eager to try new things?

✔ Is he emotionally stable and basically healthy?

✔ Is his life full and balanced, including fun, work, and learning?

If you can answer "yes" to these questions, your child is on his way to a wonderful, happy life following his passions.

Looking toward the Future

If you are like most parents, you worry about how your child will make a living. A huge challenge for a parent of a brilliant child is to balance your practical anxieties with your child's dreams. You want your child to follow her passions, of course. But what if she is a Melody Maker? Can she really make a living singing and playing the guitar in her band? Do you know the odds of a band actually making money? Do you know the lifestyle that bands lead when they are on the road? The music industry is constantly changing, and artists can't just get contracts with record labels like they once did "back in the day." It was hard then, but at least there was a clear path.

As a parent, all of these fears are likely to run through your head all of the time. You try not to interfere with your child's interests and let her have these precious high school years to explore this part of herself, but you are very careful not to allow it to overtake her life. You recognize that her grades are the most important thing, and you make sure she knows that if even one grade slips, the music will have to go. After all, it's not like she's going to major in "rock band" in college or anything, right?

This is very flawed thinking. First of all, career paths in general are not what they used to be for anyone. Many in-demand jobs now didn't even exist 10 or even five years ago.[48] There are very few jobs today that actually have corresponding college majors. Even the ones that do are not what they used to be. Take the teaching profession as an example. Years ago, it was very clear how to become a teacher. You went to a state teachers college for four years, did what was called student teaching, and got a job at the local school district afterward. While that traditional path is still available today, you can also go through alternate routes after earning a degree in almost anything else. Most states offer programs allowing college graduates to take classes in pedagogy and child development while actually working in the field. Large nonprofit organizations now offer fellowships for people who enter the teaching profession later in life. Large charter school organizations have boot camp-style programs for promising young graduates to work in their systems.

Additionally, teachers have many more options after entering the profession. Traditionally, the only career ladder option for a teacher was to become a principal. Now, teachers do all kinds of things. They become mentors for other teachers, policy advisors, curriculum developers, trainers for corporations, sales consultants for educational companies, and a host of other things that didn't exist when I became a teacher in 1984. The truth is that even in one of our most traditional professions, such as teaching, there are a multitude of jobs that were not available just a short time ago. So if your child has a passion to teach but you are worried that she won't earn enough money in that career, you are being shortsighted. If she has the desire to make money, she can follow a path within that field that will be challenging, exciting, and rewarding. She will find her way—and have a whole lot of fun doing it!

Parents also need to be cautious not to impose their hopes and dreams onto their children, who may have very different interests. A friend of mine has a son whom he believed was a Warrior. This kid was amazing when he was young. Every top sports college wanted to recruit him for at least two sports. There seemed to be no stopping him. His father was thrilled because this young man was beginning to achieve the success that had eluded the father in his youth. He put his young Warrior into every training opportunity possible. He took him to the gym and worked out with him every morning. He introduced him to pros in the area who agreed to mentor him. Their whole lives revolved around sports, and it appeared that the son would indeed fulfill the father's dream of making it to the big leagues.

But then one day, just a couple of months before he was set to begin college on a full scholarship, the boy quit. Everything. He no longer wanted to be an athlete. In fact, it turns out that he never really wanted to be an athlete in the first place. He was just doing it to make his father happy, but he couldn't stand the thought of having to make such a dedicated commitment in order to pay for college.

This father thought he had given his son the tools to succeed, but he hadn't. He had pushed and insisted and managed every aspect of his son's life and athletic career. He had failed to consider what his son really wanted, thus also failing to allow his son the opportunity to discover and develop his own interests. As a parent, you must help your child follow his own passions and nurture his desire to develop his own brilliance.

Selecting and Experiencing College

College for most teens should be preparation for life, not just a career. Although there are some students who are ready to pick a major right after high school and select a particular college or university based on their chosen major, most adolescents are not. Unfortunately, however, many parents and educators force teens to make decisions about their life's work, and then to select a college based on that decision. Don't fall into this trap. Instead, help your brilliant child select a college by discussing the following questions:

- ✔ *Is there a particular part of the country where you have always wanted to live? Are there colleges or universities there?*

- ✔ *Do you prefer a bustling city, rural area, or college town?*

- ✔ *Do you want a large campus with tens of thousands of students, where you can enjoy some anonymity and more diversity in opportunity? Or do you like a smaller, more intimate setting, where you will know most of your classmates and be known by most of your professors?*

✔ *What do you like to do for fun? What activities do you want to participate in at college?*

✔ *What is your passion? What do you want to do more than anything else every day?*

Once you have the answers to these questions, only consider schools that will allow your child to live where she wants to live, are the size that will work best for her, and include the activities and courses that suit her interests and passions. Of course, cost and distance from home are also important considerations, but they should come into play only after you have determined the framework created by answering the questions above.

Money and Motivation

Making money is something that we need to do in order to survive, but money is not what makes us happy. Many studies around the globe have explored the correlation between money and happiness, and the results boil down to some very simple concepts. If one has enough money to cover needs (food, clothing, shelter) and a few wants (personal possessions, vacations, and other fun experiences), happiness will be linked to the pursuit of what one feels one has been put on earth to do. However, if one does not have enough money to buy food, pay rent, and have occasional fun, the absence of money likely will cause intense dissatisfaction. The lack of money in this case may become a hindrance in one's life, causing great stress and creating a force that derails learning and discovery. Therefore, the best thing you can do to prepare your child for the financial realities of young adult life is to teach him how to live within his means.

Smart Money Management Matters

It is never too late to teach your child how to live within her means and manage her money wisely. In Chapter 9, I discussed how to instill these values into young children. Many of those principles apply to older teens and young adults as well. For instance, you should be a good money manager role model. Only buy what you can afford, and forego unnecessary items and events that are not practical for you in your current financial state. Children who see their parents making necessary sacrifices learn the benefits of conservation and delayed gratification. Talk to your teen about what you've done right and what you perhaps should have done differently to make yourself financially comfortable. Involve her in strategies to help reduce your expenses so that you have more money for important things, or so that you can save for something special, like a family vacation.

Making the Transition to Full Financial Responsibility

If your teenager already has a job, help him create a budget. Talk about strategies he can use to manage his money, like online and automatic bill paying, establishing separate savings accounts, using cash instead of debit cards, keeping a log of expenditures, or creating cash envelopes to manage money for incidentals. If he requires more assistance, sit down with him weekly and plan out everything that needs to happen.

If you have a college student, set up a bank account at a bank that has branches both near your home and near his college. Use the same strategy that you used with him in high school by providing a monthly allowance. If you can, when he first goes away to school, pay for his dorm or apartment ahead of time. You can also set up a meal plan that provides unlimited food or a set number of meals so you will be assured that he won't go hungry. Then have him use the money in his bank account for books, supplies, clothes, and a little entertainment. As before, if he gets into trouble, don't bail him out. If you have paid ahead for his rent and food, he will not become homeless or go hungry. You want him to have just enough so that he will learn to manage his money, but he won't have a lot of financial stress on top of all of the other adjustments he must make in the first year of college. After a successful semester or two, you may want to discuss modifying meal plans, providing him with more freedom and flexibility. Gradually, you want him to reach a point of buying his own groceries and preparing his own meals, but this doesn't need to happen right away.

Encourage your young adult to limit financial commitments so that he will not be shackled by debt while he is trying to obtain an education. Teach him to be cautious about signing up for car loans or credit cards when he is young.

Providing a Car

Transportation is an area of life that causes a great deal of difficulty for young adults. Parents sometimes purchase cars for their teens, in some cases even before they obtain their driver's licenses. Soon the teen goes off to college, taking the car with her in the belief that she'll need it to get around. However, parents should consider whether providing a teen with her own car is the best idea. Many parents do this because it is convenient for them, but your teen may be better off having to coordinate transportation with you and not having so much freedom so soon. If you do choose to provide a car, be careful to not take out too large of a loan. A loan will quickly become a burden for your child in the event that you can't or won't continue to pay on it. I have watched kids drop out of college in order to pay off their car loans. This is not a responsibility your child needs yet.

When it is time for your teen to go to college, consider not sending the car to school with her—at least, not right away. Look for schools that have adequate housing and transportation systems such that your child doesn't need a vehicle. Having a car at school increases the likelihood that she will get distracted by taking road trips with friends or returning home too frequently. You want your college student to become immersed in college life and learn to get around by walking, biking, and using public transportation.

Planning the Next Move

When it is time for your now-adult child to make the transition out of college, think about his next steps. Most kids will return to the safety of the nest as they plan their next move. The problem is that there may not be ample opportunities for them where you live. The result will be a young adult living with you and floundering for years because he can't find a job that will pay enough for him to leave home and live independently in the area where you live. Help your young adult consider some alternatives. Is there a city that has more opportunities available? Does he have any friends living in such a place who may want a roommate? Help him explore all of the options before making the assumption that the only way for him to live is with you.

My son went to Florida State University and graduated with a dual degree in theater and English. When he was ready to graduate, we lived in a suburb outside of Tampa. Daniel's dream was to become a playwright—not a field that offers instant jobs with high salaries. So he decided that he would do some type of office administration while he was exploring various opportunities in the arts. Tampa is not exactly a thriving arts community, so he wasn't crazy about moving back in with us. Further, if he *had* moved in with us, he would have needed a car, since we lived in an area not well served by public transportation and my husband and I only had one car between us. So we encouraged him to think about other options.

At the same time, many of Daniel's friends from FSU were having the same dilemma. Several of them had visited Chicago and enjoyed the fringe theater scene there. They decided that this might be a good place to be as young college grads. Four of them rented a house together and made the move. We parents helped by co-signing on their first lease, helping them furnish the place, and giving them a little seed money. Within weeks, all of the roommates were able to find work as temps in offices, and they eventually found full-time jobs. They do what they can to keep their expenses low, and there have only been a few instances when any of them has asked for financial assistance. Since then, they have created their own theater company to gain the experience in the arts that is propelling them forward. Little by little, each one is earning more money and moving closer to his ultimate goals. Each year, a few more FSU theater graduates make the move to Chicago, and they are now able to support each other as a group as they transition to living in a big city.

The Problem with Plans

Americans change jobs frequently. On average, people hold 11 different jobs between the ages of 18 and 44, according to the U.S. Department of Labor.[49] Although there is little consensus on what constitutes a career change, it seems that many of us will change careers at least a couple of times in our lifetime. So the idea of working at one job, or even in one profession, for one's lifetime is highly unlikely. Although many of us will stay in the same field, the world is changing so rapidly that we are able to explore many different types of jobs within that field. To get an understanding of this, consider the following jobs that did not exist just 10 years ago:[50]

- ✔ *Blogger:* This is someone who hosts an online web journal, filled with content that others want to read. Not only will good bloggers attract advertisers to their blog pages, they can also sell their own products or services or create affiliate networks.

- ✔ *Community Manager or Content Manager:* These managers act as a liaison between a company and the public, managing a website and publicizing the company.

- ✔ *Green Funeral Director:* Funeral directors can now incorporate environmentally friendly options to meet the needs of families who want a "green" service.

- ✔ *Interior Redesigner:* These designers remodel your home using the things you already have, either repurposing them for other uses or putting them in other rooms.

- ✔ *Patient Advocate:* There are several types of patient advocates, and although their services vary, all of them want to make sure that the patient and family are informed, as well as to make things easier on everyone. Advocates can go with patients to appointments, ensure that they're visiting with the right specialists and taking the right medicines, sort through medical bills and negotiate fees with health-care providers and insurance companies, and even educate family members on the proper care for their sick loved one.

✔ *Senior Move Manager:* These people help older adults and families with the physical and emotional demands of downsizing, relocating, or modifying their homes.

✔ *Social Media Strategists:* Using social media tools, these strategists help companies interact with customers, increase brand awareness, create buzz, increase traffic, and provide information.

✔ *User Experience Analyst:* These individuals look for ways to make using a website easier, more pleasant, and more engaging for consumers. They want to figure out how to keep you on a particular site and how to make your experience while you're there memorable and useful.

✔ *Video Journalist:* These small-market reporters produce, shoot, and edit their own stories, often to provide content that will drive web traffic.

✔ *Virtual Business Service Provider:* Many people are forming their own companies by way of telecommuting, offering such virtual services as customer service, concierge services, or even public relations from their homes.

It's hard to imagine what jobs might be available 10 years in the future. How do you help a young person prepare for a career that doesn't even exist yet? Instead of thinking about education as job preparation, think of it as life preparation. Allow the college years to be about exploring one's passions, developing skills in communication, thinking, and collaboration. You are investing in your child's mind and soul, not her financial worth.

Jordan is a Designer, and she decided that she wanted to study art—specifically painting and drawing—in college. So when it was time to choose a college, Jordan searched for one that had a good fine arts department. When she and her mother toured colleges, Jordan's eyes lit up when she walked into the art studios and saw all of the artists at work. She knew that she wanted to be a part of this world. When her mother asked her what in the world she would do with an art degree, Jordan could not answer her; she really didn't know what happens to people who study art and how they are able to live after college. Jordan's mother tried to persuade her to think about advertising or graphic arts designing packaging, but Jordan wanted to paint. She couldn't think about art in terms of a computer screen and commercial applications.

Jordan's mother simply would not allow her daughter to major in art. If she was going to pay the enormous tuition required for Jordan to attend a private college, she was going to get her money's worth. She told Jordan that she could minor in art, but she must major in something "practical." Since she had also done well in science in high school, Jordan ended up being a biology major. Although she was less than completely enthusiastic about her choice of major, she thought she'd at least be able to finally study figure drawing and begin her painting classes. Unfortunately, this did not happen. It turned out that freshmen were not allowed to take such classes in the art department unless they were majoring in the subject. Jordan would have to wait until her sophomore year, and even then there were not many seats available for non-majors.

So Jordan took courses to fulfill her general education requirements and scheduled a couple of biology classes to begin working toward her major. She never connected with anyone at college, and by the middle of the spring semester, she just stopped going to class, although she didn't reveal this to her mother. Finally, at the beginning of May, she let her mother know that she would not be returning to college, but would instead move back home.

Jordan's mother was devastated. She couldn't understand why her daughter, who had always been a good student, was dropping out of college. Jordan eventually began attending a technical school and learned to be a medical technician. Later, she started taking art classes in the evenings and is now working on some art projects outside of her job to fulfill her creative needs.

Jordan is a Designer and will always be a Designer. But instead of having an opportunity to explore this part of herself in the wonderful environment of college art studios, she ended up in a job she hates, trying to figure out how to get back to doing what she loves.

So what do you want for your child? Do you want her to be passionate about her area of brilliance and do all she can to follow her passions? Or do you want her to lead a practical life and fit in the other stuff in small ways when she can? It is absolutely possible to lead a life of purpose and fulfill one's passions. We just have to have a little courage to allow our children to be true to themselves.

Finding the Right Path

What are some career paths that a brilliant child may want to pursue as he reaches adulthood? What follows is a guide for potential college and career directions that might make this dream-following thing just a little bit less scary for you in your role as parent.

Storytellers

While most Storytellers certainly appreciate literature and creative writing, they may be interested in subjects that go beyond these, such as theater, film, anthropology, archeology, humanities, history, or anything else that focuses on stories. In addition, since the language centers of Storytellers' brains are usually highly developed, they sometimes enjoy studying other languages. Encourage them to consider any college major that will allow them to reach and grow in what interests them the most. There are plenty of practical jobs available to Storytellers, including journalism, publishing, office administration, or anything requiring writing. If they have mastered another language, they can be translators. They are highly employable in any area that incorporates language or writing.

Calculators

These are the true math brains. It's best if they can find a college that has plenty of advanced courses linked to other exciting fields of study, such as engineering and finance. They also excel at computer programming, computer repair, robotics, or anything that requires high levels of logical analysis. Upon graduation, they can often find work specific to their college preparation. If no higher-end professional positions are available, they might enjoy working as "geeks" or "geniuses" at computer stores, doing work in accounting offices, IT management, or any position that values analysis. Many Calculators will move up to higher positions as electrical or aerospace engineers, university professors, or actuaries in business.

Explorers

Explorers love anything that lets them discover and connect. They gravitate toward majors in medicine, zoology, microbiology, paleontology, geology, entomology, marine biology, and other scientific pursuits. There are lots of different science mediums, and you want your Explorer to choose the one that is most interesting to him—not necessarily the one with the best employment options. After graduation, Explorers can find work in hospitals, research labs, animal and natural resource management, or even food safety and analysis. They generally like jobs that allow them to complete assigned tasks with autonomy and work to increase efficiency.

Magnets

Magnets are drawn to careers where they can be leaders or influence others. They tend to major in public policy, law, education, political science, and business management. However, they should be encouraged to pursue a companion major in something that will be fun for them so their skills can be put to work in fields that engage their interest. It is best if they attend a school that has plenty of leadership opportunities for them so that they can hone their abilities before they launch into the job market. These young adults are easily employable because people are so drawn to them.

They are usually good at sales and can also excel in management, law, politics, public relations, and human resources.

Designers

There are lots of different types of Designers, so it is important to understand which medium calls to them. Although a Designer may change her medium of choice over the course of her career, it is critical to allow her to pursue the one that ignites her passion while in college. Options include painting, sculpting, architecture, animation, gaming design, graphic design, interior design, or fashion design. Pay attention to your Designer's tendencies, and be sure the college you choose offers plenty of opportunities to pursue her particular passion, but that will also allow her to experiment in other mediums if she broadens or alters her viewpoint. Allow her to choose a college and art or design major that will work for her.

Once college is over, Designers can find work in a variety of fields, including web creation, advertising, graphic design, illustration, and management of establishments that provide arts experiences to others. They can also find work in museums, design houses, and architecture firms, allowing them to be surrounded by what they love.

Melody Makers

Melody Makers like anything to do with music, and they usually have good math brains, too. They might major in music, music production, music history, or anything else dealing with music. Melody Makers who develop skills in piano or percussion can usually find work in larger cities as accompanists or standing in for bands. They tend to be performers and are usually good at any job that involves customer service and interacting with the public.

Butterflies

Butterflies combine the need to move with musical and artistic sensibility. They need a college experience that allows them to be artistically expressive and to keep moving. They typically major in dance, fine arts with opportunities to keep dancing, or events planning. Most Butterflies also enjoy storytelling and can excel in the areas similar to those favored by Storytellers. However, they need constant opportunities during college to continue their love of dance or movement. Upon graduation, and even while in college, Butterflies can find work at dance studios, at after-school programs, and working for arts organizations in a variety of capacities. They may also enjoy working within sports organizations that incorporate dance, such as ice skating, gymnastics, cheerleading, and even marching bands. They often enjoy event planning that involves large flows of people, such as conventions, weddings, and parades.

Charmers

Charmers love attention and should study areas that put them in the spotlight. These include mass communication and acting. They also often enjoy performing in music, comedy, and some sports. While Charmers are in college, they generally want to pursue things that satisfy their need to be noticed. This might be in areas such as theater or film, or in sorority or fraternity positions. Charmers prefer colleges where they can be more of a big fish in a little pond. Look for smaller schools with smaller classes where your Charmer can become the center of attention quickly. Think about schools that value her particular talents and passions so she can easily become a part of the action.

Remember, there is a difference between Charmers and Magnets. Charmers are performers, while Magnets are leaders. A Charmer will enjoy a career in which she is watched and appreciated, and even idolized a bit. A Magnet wants to draw people to him and lead them in a meaningful way. Upon graduation from college, Charmers will enjoy any position that allows them to be seen. In fact, they will sometimes struggle to work at entry-level positions in places where they want to be the star. For example, if your Charmer was a mass communications major, she may not want to work as a production assistant at a television studio. Instead, she may want to do some independent video journalism, posting content herself to build her reel while she works in a day job as a restaurant host.

Warriors

Warriors need to move. They do well in majors that require physical activity, like sports, agriculture management, equestrian training, athletic training, parks management, natural resource management, and physical therapy. The less time at a desk for a Warrior, the better. Warriors should be encouraged to participate in as many sports as possible while in college. They can join the school's competitive teams, as well as community or intramural leagues. If there are not a lot of sports teams available, they can pursue club activities in recreational sports like skiing, diving, camping, and kayaking.

Warriors can find lots of interesting work upon college graduation. They can work in national and state parks, for professional athletic teams, as trainers of all kinds of sports teams and clubs, as personal trainers in health clubs, and as youth leaders in camps or in before- and after-school programs.

Cool Combos

As you have been reading this book, you may have wondered to yourself, "What about children who seem to have strong passions in more than one area of brilliance? What about the child who loves both music and dance? Or both science and language? How do we guide children with several areas of brilliance?" The answer is that interests and passions can oftentimes be combined.

Most brilliant people have more than one area in which they can excel. It is exciting to recognize combinations that can lead to unusual futures. Allison Hooper had a love of the French language and for agriculture, which led to a wonderful career making cheese.

People who forecast the weather on television combine the qualities of a Charmer with those of an Explorer. Designers who are also Calculators might become architects or transportation planners or video game designers. Butterflies who are also Storytellers may find success in theater or choreography. Magnets who are also Warriors make great athletic coaches or managers, while a Magnet who is also a Melody Maker might become a conductor, performer, or music producer. There are many careers that result from a combination of two or more passions or areas of brilliance.

The key to helping your brilliant child create a fulfilling life is to give him the time and space to explore his passions and an education that prepares him for life. While he is still getting his education, teach him how to handle the practical details of his life, like managing time, money, food, and shelter, and help him arrange his life so that he can live independently and within his means.

Parents often unwittingly snuff out brilliance by worrying about life's practical realities. It is not uncommon to hear a parent say something like, "That music stuff is all well and good, but it's not like you can make any money at it." As soon as a child demonstrates brilliance in an area not readily equated with financial success, it is typical for adults to become concerned. The truth is that following one's passions can and does lead to career success. Each area of brilliance is a flame that can burn brightly. Risks need to be taken, and passions need to be followed in order for brilliant children to lead brilliant lives.

CHAPTER 11

The Spectrum: Profiles of Brilliance

Sometime during the 2008 presidential election, democratic candidate Barack Obama was accused of being "elite" and "intellectual." These adjectives were used in a negative, derogatory way, implying that someone who is brilliant is somehow inferior to more common folk. Republican candidate for vice president Sarah Palin capitalized on her folksy way of communicatin' and reminded us all that she was just a "hockey mom" from Alaska. This was not a new way to differentiate between candidates. We saw it before in the election with candidates Ronald Reagan and George W. Bush. But somehow in 2008, being smart got a really bad rap. We had "Joe the Plumber" telling us who to vote for, and the rhetoric centered around the desire to elect someone who was "one of us."

Throughout this, I kept thinking, "I want a really smart president. I want someone whose intellect would allow him or her to solve the incredibly complex problems of our country and our world." *Average* is not a word I would want to use to describe someone in a top leadership position in a company, let alone as a leader of our country.

It should be no surprise that we have become satisfied with mediocrity in our schools. Our goal has become to get students to reach designated benchmarks at each grade level, never considering the wonderful differences and potential among individual children. Psychologist James T. Webb, expert on issues affecting brilliant children, states, "In our current school systems, mediocrity, conformity, and fitting in are more valued than innovation, excellence, and creativity."[51] Our goal should be to help every child be the most he or she can possibly be instead of simply reaching a one-size-fits-all level of proficiency.

What if there weren't any brilliant people? Where would we be without the progress made possible by the spectrum of amazing contributions of the Wright brothers, Henry Ford, Thomas Edison, Madame Curie, Susan B. Anthony, Martin Luther King, Jr., Norma Rae, César Chávez, Maya Angelou, and others? Our world is a better place because of the contributions of these people, and we should do all we can to encourage great achievement among our brilliant children. Your job as a parent is to raise incredible young adults who will give the world all of their brilliance and create happy, full lives of their own in the process. Think about all you are doing to create an environment that promotes development and that will allow these children to truly reach their potential.[52]

An Average Life

My grandparents had what most people would consider an average life. They were wonderful, amazing people who chose to live a very typical American suburban existence. My grandfather served proudly in World War II as a Merchant Marine, while my grandmother held down the fort at home, working in a defense plant and raising their two children. When my grandfather came back from the war, she dutifully stepped back into her role as full-time mom and directed her energies toward volunteer activities in the community. They both instilled a solid work ethic into their children, and eventually their grandchildren. We always appreciated how hard they worked, how they saved and planned and gave back to the community. From my grandparents have come three more generations of people who share solid American values and contribute much to society. Another generation is just beginning, and they will no doubt benefit from the continuance of this family legacy.

There is certainly nothing wrong with my ordinary grandparents. I am proud to be their descendant and have passed along their values to my children. They both led happy, long lives and relished the ordinariness of it all. Simple things like walking along the beach, having Sunday dinners, and celebrating birthdays were the best things in life for them. But they always encouraged the brilliance in all of their children, grandchildren, and great grandchildren. They were the biggest supporters of all of our endeavors, and they were so proud of each of our accomplishments. We have Melody Makers, Storytellers, Calculators, and all of the other areas of brilliance within our family, and my grandparents recognized these talents and preferred areas of interest in all of us. They wanted us to be the very best we could possibly be, and they encouraged us to become extraordinary.

Sometimes brilliant children come from brilliant parents, and sometimes they come from more humble origins. But with the right encouragement and the right circumstances, along with drive, persistence, resilience, and talent, brilliant children can become brilliant adults who contribute to the betterment of our world. Take a look at some famous and not-so-famous people who have capitalized on their areas of brilliance to create wonderful lives.

Profiles of Brilliance

Storytellers

The Nobel Prize and Pulitzer Prize have both been awarded to one of the great Storytellers of our time, Toni Morrison. From a very young age, Toni reveled in stories, first from listening to her father tell them, and then by writing down her own. Toni is the author of defining works of fiction, including *The Bluest Eye* and

Beloved. Her works have made her well-known across the globe as someone who can infuse a sense of poetry into fiction, help us understand our deepest connections through her nonfiction, and inspire others in her work as a college professor and editor. Toni honed her skills as a Storyteller through formal education, first at Howard University, where she earned a Bachelor of Arts in English, and later at Cornell with a Master's in English.

Like Toni Morrison, Barbara Martinez is fascinated by stories, but she focuses her storytelling on institutions that impact our daily lives. In her reporting for the *Wall Street Journal*, she shines a light on the business of healthcare, real estate, and education. Her preparation for this career started with a journalism degree from New York University. Now, as a mother, she works in her own community to improve educational opportunities for children. Barbara is an excellent listener who works to find the truth about the things that matter to us all. She uses her storytelling abilities to share information so that others can join in making the world a better place.

Calculators

Math is an elegant way to solve problems. Someone who understood this well was Edith Clark, who lived from 1883 to 1959. After losing both parents at age 12, Edith used the inheritance they left her to go to college at age 18. This was not the standard practice for women at the dawn of the 20th century, but off Edith went to Vassar to study mathematics and astronomy. After graduating in 1908, she settled into a career that was a little more traditional: teaching at a private girls' school, and later at Marshall College in West Virginia. But this did not satisfy Edith, and she soon began studying engineering at the University of Wisconsin. After a summer job as a computing assistant (the human kind) at AT&T, Edith was hooked and decided to stay on full time.

A Calculator in more modern times, Glenn Fuir studied economics, accounting, and business management in college. He soon began making his way in the banking industry, focusing on accounting practices. Having an insatiable appetite for more knowledge, Glenn continued his education by getting a Master's in Business Administration, as well as several financial management certifications along the way. He went into financial forecasting, worked to improve credit practices at various financial institutions, and now works at the Federal Reserve, ensuring sound practices in credit and risk management for financial institutions.

Glenn has combined his amazing math abilities with outstanding people skills to become an exceptional manager in an industry that is vital to our country's future. His solid foundation in math and logic led him to making an important impact in the Federal Reserve. Like many Calculators, Glenn also enjoys music. You can often find him playing one of his numerous guitars and rehearsing with friends in a band.

Explorers

It takes a rocket scientist to solve the problems that occur in space, and Guion "Guy" Bluford, Jr., was up to the challenge when he became the first African-American astronaut to go to space. Guy was able to exercise his problem-solving skills early in his life by going through the ranks of the Boy Scouts, eventually attaining the coveted rank of Eagle Scout by earning multiple badges and completing a community service project. He earned a B.S. in Aerospace Engineering from Penn State and then became a pilot in the Air Force, flying 144 missions in Vietnam in just two years. He soon continued his formal education, earning a Master's and then a Doctorate in Aerospace Engineering from the Air Force Institute of Technology. Within a year of earning his Ph.D., Guy was selected by NASA to become an astronaut, and he became the first African-American in space, aboard the Challenger in 1983. His specialty was operating the robotic arm, which was critical to success on those missions involving SpaceLab. After a truly stellar career as an astronaut, logging 688 hours in space, Guy entered civilian life in 1993, working for a Department of Defense contractor.

I am thankful for a lesser-known Explorer who has been my personal physician. Donna M. Mendes, M.D., is a nationally and internationally recognized vascular surgeon. As an African-American woman, she is continually trying to solve the vascular problems that tend to affect the African-American community. She is also nurturing a renewed interest in venous disease pathology and treatment. As a member of the Society of Black American Surgeons, Dr. Mendes mentors young women interested in pursuing a career in surgery and has received numerous letters requesting guidance from as far away as Nigeria. Even though she has a very busy practice, she finds time to volunteer in the community and to continue her efforts to explore and discover new drugs and procedures that may help her patients. She is living a remarkable and fulfilling life through her commitment to science and to helping people.

Magnets

César Chávez quit school after completing eighth grade so that he could help his family by earning money as a migrant farm worker. He took a break to join the military, but after a brief stint there, he returned to the fields. At the age of 25, frustrated and angered by the social injustices affecting Mexican-Americans in California, César became an organizer for the Community Service Organization. Immediately identified as someone who could make an impact, he was hired and trained by Fred Ross to help in the efforts to combat police brutality. Through his influence, César convinced many Latinos to register and vote. Ten years later, he co-founded the National Farm Workers Association, which eventually became the United Farm Workers. Through the efforts of this group, working conditions and wages improved for farm workers in California and Florida. César is celebrated today as a hero for Latinos and for laborers. He was a true Magnet, able to inspire others and lead them to help change their world.

Another Magnet of notable influence, Derrell Bradford has become a major voice for school reform in New Jersey and beyond. His goal when he was Executive Director of E3 was to break the monopoly of public education. A Storyteller early in life, Derrell earned a B.A. in English and Creative Writing from the University of Pennsylvania, but he was drawn to the education reform movement, just as Chávez was drawn to his cause. Derrell is incensed by the injustice of our educational system and wants to lead others to bring long-lasting change. His efforts are gaining traction, as New Jersey works to become one of the leaders of school choice. School choice includes a wide variety of options for children, including attending a different school within their own district; attending a school in a different district; using virtual school, independent learning, and distance education options; attending a charter school; and receiving a scholarship to be used at a private school. The bottom line is that parents should be empowered to make educational choices that are in the best interest of each individual child. The quality of a child's education should not be determined by zip code, and Derrell uses both his Magnet and his Storytelling abilities to educate the public about this critical issue. You can find him at community events promoting school choice and on national news shows rallying support across the country.

Designers

Georgia O'Keeffe's parents valued education for girls in the early 20th century, when it was not expected by society. They required their daughters to become educated, and also to take art lessons, where it was discovered that Georgia had significant talent. From there, they provided her with the best instruction in art, coupled with a solid academic foundation. At one point, Georgia became frustrated by her experiences as an artist and left the field to become an elementary school teacher. But like most Designers, she simply couldn't abandon her art and found her way back quickly. It didn't take long for the art world to notice her, resulting in record-breaking prices for her work in 1923. Georgia eventually settled in New Mexico, and you can view much of her work at a museum in Santa Fe, thanks to her careful estate planning.

Georgia led an extraordinary life, especially for someone who came of age at a time when women were not encouraged to become accomplished in anything other than managing a household. Her parents' insistence that she and her sisters become educated and attend art classes certainly made this possible.

My good friend Adrienne "Adi" Haspel is a video editor for PBS in New York City. She is a Designer who uses video as her medium. Adi always had the soul of a Designer, but she started out in life as a Butterfly, dancing her way across her native Hungary. As she grew older, she realized that her life as a dancer would not last forever, so she started exploring other areas that fueled her passion for life, such as photography and film editing. She knew that she needed technical skills for these endeavors, so she enrolled in New York University's editing program and learned what she needed to know to get started in this competitive field.

Adi loves what she does because she gets to learn so much about the topic of each documentary she works on. Not every video editor is a Designer; many of them bring more of a logical context to their work, seeing the work more as following the lead of the director. But while Adi certainly wants to be true to the director's vision, her own artistry makes her work intense and vibrant, no matter what the subject. One of her recent projects, a documentary about a famous Hungarian dancer, allowed Adi to merge all of the parts of herself into one glorious work. She sees the beauty in all that is around her and focuses her life's work on bringing the world to life for others.

Melody Makers

Anne Akiko Meyers got her start on the *Tonight Show* with Johnny Carson when she was just 11 years old. Her early years playing chamber music no doubt contributed to her success. Today she is an enormously successful classical musician, touring the world with one of her two Stradivarius violins. She made quite a buzz when she bought her second Stradivarius—for a reported 3.6 million dollars.

Anne has always followed her passion of music since seeing a violinist on stage at the Hollywood Bowl when she was just seven years old. After that, she knew what she wanted to do. She frequently states how lucky she feels, being able to speak to the world through the universal language of music. Her parents supported her dream by providing her with an excellent musical education. She studied as a child at the Colburn School of Performing Arts in Los Angeles, and later, she continued her studies at Indiana University and Juilliard. Now she touches the hearts and souls of others through her music, certainly inspiring some of them to follow their passions in the same way that she became inspired by listening to a brilliant musician herself.

There are many Melody Makers who don't make a worldwide splash and don't have quite enough money for a Stradivarius, but they contribute greatly to the culture and well-being of our communities just the same. You have probably never heard of Stuart Kollmorgen and Matt Pedone, but you and your children may have heard some of their music. Stuart and Matt are the founding partners of The Big Yellow Duck, a company that specializes in sound design and audio post services. After attending the Berklee School of Music, Stuart began his career as a musical director, working with then-unknowns like The Blue Man Group and John Leguizamo. Matt, after graduating from Syracuse University, toured as a drummer before going into advertisement and media production. Eventually, the two joined forces to create the sounds for shows like *Johnny and the Sprites*, *Stanley*, and *Jojo's Circus* for the Disney Channel, as well as *Kenny the Shark* for Discovery Kids.

If you go into Stuart's office today, you will see an impressive collection of guitars and other instruments alongside his computer editing equipment. If you are really lucky, you might get a chance to hear Matt on the drums outside of the office. These two Melody Makers are wonderful examples of people who have followed their passions without hesitation. As Stuart says, "There is nothing I'd rather do than what I'm doing right now. I have been in this business for 20 years, and I feel as juiced about the next project as I did about the first."[53]

Butterflies

Darci Kistler was born to dance. As the only girl in a family with four boys, she was exposed to lots of rough-and-tumble sports. But at the age of four, after seeing a professional ballet performance, she asked her mother if she could take ballet lessons. Darci could not get enough of ballet, and at age 16, she earned a spot at the School of American Ballet, where George Ballanchine, co-founder of the New York City Ballet, taught. He was immediately impressed with the young Butterfly and made her a principal dancer with the New York City Ballet when she was just 17 years old, the youngest dancer ever to perform in that company. Darci danced with the New York City Ballet for 30 years and continued on as a teacher after that. This true Butterfly has danced her way through life.

Another Butterfly who is far less famous is Florence Geise. Now at a time of life when most of her contemporaries have retired, Florence is a hard-working dance and humanities teacher at the Renaissance Academy near Tampa, Florida. As a young dancer, Florence was attracted by the bright lights of New York City, and she moved there from her rural Pennsylvania town, ultimately working as a professional ballerina for the Radio City Music Hall Ballet Company. Later, she returned to her hometown and created a nonprofit organization that provides opportunities for young dancers in the community. While doing so, Florence earned a bachelor's degree and master's degree and turned her love of humanities, communication, and dance into a unique career at a school that integrates the arts and academics. She never slows down and has remarked on more than one occasion that she wants to be buried with her dance shoes on.

Charmers

Mario Lopez is an actor, television host, dancer, producer, and fitness author, but all of these things became possible for him because he is a Charmer. You just can't take your eyes off of him if he is on the stage or on screen. People who know him want to be near him and watch him make magic happen.

Mario was born in San Diego and began his career as an actor at the tender age of 11 on the television show *A.K.A. Pablo*. He was also a drummer and dancer on *Kids Incorporated*. He continued his formal education and was a champion wrestler in high school. Throughout his high school years, he worked as an actor, making appearances on *The Golden Girls* and starring in the tween/teen hit *Saved by the Bell*. After graduating in 1991, Mario continued pursuing his professional career. He has worked steadily since, including roles on both the large and small screens. He has added to his resume entertainment show host, *Dancing with the Stars* dancer, boxing commentator, and Broadway actor. Most recently, he authored a fitness book called *Knockout Fitness*, complete with a shirtless photo of him on the cover.

A Charmer doesn't have to be famous to make an impact. You can find them in many different professions, including public advocacy. Roscoe Wilson began his professional life as a basketball player working in Sweden and Argentina. After leaving the world of pro sports, he longed to make a difference in his own community, and so he began working as an instructor for a nonprofit organization serving troubled youth. It didn't take long for Roscoe to get noticed, and he quickly moved up through the ranks of the organization.

What is amazing about Roscoe is how many people recognize this non-famous man. At 6'6" tall with a booming voice, he is hard to miss. But just in case you might, he can often be seen in cowboy boots and a large cowboy hat, as a nod to his Texas roots. I have walked through airports, legislative halls, and shopping malls with Roscoe in Florida, California, Texas, Arkansas, Delaware, and the Cayman Islands. Everywhere we go, someone recognizes him. Old, young, male and female, all ethnic backgrounds—people know Roscoe. He is not famous, and yet somehow he is. He is a Charmer of the largest proportions, able to influence people with a nod or a quick grin or joke. Roscoe has been a guest at the White House twice but is just as comfortable at a pig roast fund raiser for a local politician. His combination of commitment to education and public service certainly come from his parents, who were accomplished in both arenas. He earned his bachelor's degree at Benedict College in South Carolina and continued with his graduate studies in Sweden.

Today Roscoe is using his Charmer status to influence public policy related to juvenile justice and education issues around the United States. It is wonderful to see someone of Roscoe's stature using his powers for the greatest good imaginable: taking care of our kids!

Warriors

Peyton and Eli Manning are two of the most successful football players in the NFL. Sons of Archie Manning, who was also an NFL player, the boys began playing football early. The Manning family ensured the success of their sons by creating a balanced home life and stressing the values of hard work and perseverance. Both young Warriors earned college degrees and made choices about who would coach them based on their own improvement needs at each decision point. Although their parents were pleased that the boys shared their father's love of football, the Manning family nurtured their boys in a way that encouraged and developed their talent, allowing that talent to be part of who they are but not everything they are.

You may know of Warriors in your community who relish every moment when they can be involved in highly physically challenging endeavors. Hugh "Skip" Gibson, who also happens to be my cousin, is one of those Warriors. When we were growing up in New Jersey, Skip loved many different sports, excelling at swimming and football. As a teenager, he worked as a beach lifeguard on the Jersey shore. Never one to be satisfied with a sedentary lifestyle, Skip began volunteering as a firefighter, which he did for several years before obtaining a paid firefighter position. After 26 years, having been Chief Fire Marshall and Battalion Chief, Skip retired from firefighting and now works with the Insurance Service Organization, assisting local fire chiefs and commissioners in utilizing data to calculate insurance rates and reduce taxes for local municipalities.

Throughout his adult life, Skip has also been a professional referee for high school and NCAA college football. Literally the picture of a Warrior, Skip assisted an illustrator friend by modeling for illustrations of several GI Joe action figures. This productive, happy life was made possible by Skip's attention to his education and his preparation for his future. He continually took advantage of educational opportunities surrounding his passion for football and firefighting, completing a degree in fire science administration and continuing to hone his skills in his profession through his work as an adjunct instructor at a local college.

What Will Your Child Contribute to the World?

All of the examples in this chapter demonstrate lives well lived because each individual followed his or her passions in each area of brilliance. What a privilege it was for my husband and me to enjoy sharing our home with a Storyteller and a Melody Maker! They filled our lives with imagination and music, and they continue to inspire us today. Maybe you are lucky enough to be chasing after a Butterfly or Warrior who will certainly keep you on the move! Perhaps you are enjoying answering the amazing questions that your Explorer poses, marveling at how your Calculator makes sense out of chaos, or seeing the world through your Designer's eyes. Or you might be basking in the glory of your Magnet or Charmer, wondering what adventures lie ahead.

The type of brilliance is not important. Enjoy every moment. Create those sparks. Provide an inspiring education and opportunities to develop self-discipline. Use your child's strengths to even out the rough spots. Ensure that he or she is surrounded by encouragement to accomplish, as well as a positive peer group. Intervene when there is an issue that needs to be addressed. Create a world where passions are celebrated and brilliance is truly nurtured!

Parents of brilliant children have a particular responsibility to raise them in a way that will benefit the world. As John F. Kennedy said, "For those to whom much is given, much is required." It can be daunting when you first realize how special your child is. You may feel that you do not have adequate skills to raise a child like this. Don't worry; you can do it. With a little thought and intention, you will be successful. Certainly, you will make mistakes. Every parent does. The totality of your child's upbringing is what is important. You can create a childhood filled with wonder, opportunity, and exploration that feeds the soul of your brilliant child, while also providing a solid structure for development. As long as you provide this context, the details will take care of themselves.

There is so much that brilliant children, and the adults they will become, can offer the world—a whole spectrum of possibilities. Brilliant children can grow up to lead truly extraordinary, happy lives, and we can all benefit from their gifts.

Endnotes

1   Elementary and Secondary Education Act, Title IX, Part A, Definition 22 (2002).

2   National Association for Gifted Children, 2010

3   Gardner, 1983. Gardner's theories were built on earlier work by psychologists Spearman and Thurstone (Hockenbury & Hockenbury, 2011).

4   Sometimes people use terms like "rapid learner," "advanced learner," "talented," or "high potential" as substitute words.

5   If you are concerned about your child's education, there are many good resources available for more information on how to advocate effectively in the educational arena. To learn more, you may want to consult the following books and websites: *Academic Advocacy for Gifted Children* by Barbara J. Gilman; *Re-Forming Gifted Education* by Karen Rogers; *A Parent's Guide to Gifted Children* by James T. Webb, Janet L. Gore, Edward R. Amend, and Arlene R DeVries; *Helping Gifted Children Soar* by Carol Ann Strip and Gretchen Hirsch; *A Parent's Guide to Gifted Teens* by Lisa Rivero; the National Association for Gifted Children: www.nagc.org; Supporting Emotional Needs of the Gifted: www.sengifted.org; and Hoagies' Gifted Education Page: www.hoagiesgifted.org.

6   According to the *Handbook of Gifted Education* (Colangelo & Davis, 2002), up to one-fifth of dropouts test in the gifted range. An interesting analysis of the data can be found at http://giftedexchange.blogspot.com/2008/09/are-20-of-high-school-drop-outs-gifted.html.

7   Renzulli & Park, 2002

8   Feldman, 1984, p. 519

9   This phenomenon is described in *Understanding Creativity* by Jane Piirto.

10   Webb, 2009

11   Susan Daniels and Michael Piechowski describe this issue well in the book *Living with Intensity* (Daniels & Piechowski, Eds., 2009), and they provide readers with a clear picture of the intensity and sensitivity that brilliant children often exhibit, which are often referred to as "overexcitabilities," first defined by Polish psychologist Kazimierz Dabrowski. Dabrowski sorted gifted individuals' various seemingly extreme reactions into five categories: intellectual, emotional, imaginational, sensual, and psychomotor. Children with intellectual overexcitability seem to have an insatiable drive to learn, and they may question constantly or work intently for long periods on logic puzzles or games. Children with emotional overexcitability may form very close relationships with others and have emotional attachments to people, places, and things. Their feelings may be so intense that they have physical responses, such as headaches or stomachaches, to their emotions. Children who have imaginational overexcitability tend to be very visual, speak in metaphors, and enjoy a rich fantasy life that often includes imaginary friends or characters. Children with sensual overexcitability may be very sensitive to sights, sounds, odors, flavors, or textures. Many of these children have sensitive skin and require that you cut the tags out of their shirts, or they may complain that they are distracted by the flickering of fluorescent lights above them. Children who have psychomotor overexcitability may have boundless energy, speaking rapidly and exhibiting difficulty just sitting still.

   Another issue that contributes to a brilliant person's intensity is the concept of "flow." Psychology professor Mihaly Csikszentmihalyi described this as the state of immersion in one's work or other activity during which one becomes completely absorbed and fulfilled. In a child's area of brilliance, this state of "flow" can be experienced frequently, sometimes to the complete rejection of everything else (Csikszentmihalyi, 1990).

12   Webb, Amend, Webb, Goerss, Beljan, & Olenchak, 2005

13   One helpful resource is the book *Misdiagnosis and Dual Diagnoses of Gifted Children and Adults* by James T. Webb, Edward R. Amend,

Nadia E. Webb, Jean Goerss, Paul Beljan, and F. Richard Olenchak. For up-to-date information and support for a wide variety of emotional needs of gifted children, you may want to connect with the organization called SENG (Supporting Emotional Needs of the Gifted) at www.sengifted.org.

14   Csikszentmihalyi, 1990

15   Renzulli & Park, 2002

16   Pink, 2009

17   Psychologist Ellen Winner (1997) describes a quality in brilliant children that she refers to as a "rage to master." Children, at very early ages, will become obsessive and intense in their desire to become better at particular activities such as reading, writing, math, music, or any other area of brilliance. They will pursue activities in their chosen area to the exclusion of everything else, in isolation of other people.

18   Sometimes homeschooling can be the best option for brilliant children, offering more freedom to pursue an area of brilliance without wasting time on things they have already mastered. Parents who wish to homeschool their children should plan properly and use all available resources to ensure the best experience possible for their children. Lisa Rivero provides guidance and information on this important topic in her book *Creative Home Schooling: A Resource Guide for Smart Families.*

19   Advocating for your child in any educational setting is important. You want your child to get every advantage possible and receive an education that is tailored to his or her individual needs. To learn how to effectively leverage educational resources, see Barbara Gilman's book *Academic Advocacy for Gifted Children: A Parent's Complete Guide.*

20   Some schools are not aware of the many different ways to meet needs of gifted children. In her book *Re-Forming Gifted Education* (2002), Karen Rogers recommends that parents learn about various gifted options before approaching the school district with requests for accommodations, and she gives an overview of some 35 options in her book.

21   Gray (n.d.). Audrey Gray is a researcher from the Saskatchewan School Trustees Association specializing in teaching and learning.

22   Educational specialist Dr. Deborah Ruf distinguishes among five levels of giftedness and offers information and suggestions for understanding the needs of each group. Her distinctions are based on learning ability, as well as drive and intensity. Ruf asserts that

educational approaches need to be tailored according to these levels in order to best meet the needs of individual children. Her book *5 Levels of Gifted: School Issues and Educational Options* provides new insights into this issue.

23   As our society has become more focused on technology and parents are home less often, children have been forced indoors. It is not uncommon for a child to spend almost no time outside. This was not the case just a generation or two ago, when children were outdoors for most of the day. Richard Louv believes that much of what ails kids today, including attention problems, may be caused by a lack of connection with nature. You can learn more about this phenomenon, and how to help your child get in touch with nature, in Louv's book *Last Child in the Woods: Saving our Children from Nature-Deficit Disorder.*

24   This intensity can cause a host of emotional and behavioral issues that must be addressed in order for the child to function well. You may be interested in reading *Living with Intensity: Understanding the Sensitivity, Excitability, and Emotional Development of Gifted Children, Adolescents, and Adults,* edited by Susan Daniels and Michael M. Piechowski.

25   See Coyle, 2009, and Gladwell, 2008.

26   Gladwell's book *Outliers* is based partly on the work of K. Anders Ericsson, Ralf T. Krampe, and Clemens Tesch-Römer. Their article "The Role of Deliberate Practice in the Acquisition of Expert Performance" identifies how time devoted to a particular pursuit is required for mastery. Their research findings suggest that although a person can be born with innate abilities, time working in the chosen area is required to achieve greatness. Over and over again, the numbers 10,000 hours or 10 years seem to be identified as the threshold one must cross in order to achieve mastery of a particular skill. Daniel Levitin makes a similar case in *This Is Your Brain on Music: The Science of a Human Obsession,* as does Daniel Coyle in *The Talent Code: Greatness Isn't Born. It's Grown. Here's How.*

27   The problem of bullying has been prominent in the press in recent times. Bullying is the repeated attempt by one person or a group of people to belittle, insult, and harass another in an effort to gain power over that person. Both children and adults can become the targets of bullies. The bullying victim often feels isolated and helpless to deal with the situation. A bully can be taught to stop this destructive behavior by developing empathy for others. A victim can be taught

to stand up to a bully and avoid future victimization. To learn more about this important issue, go to www.stopbullying.gov, talk to local school and community organizations dedicated to the eradication of bullying, or read books on the topic, such as Barbara Coloroso's *The Bully, the Bullied, and the Bystander: From Preschool to High School—How Parents and Teachers Can Help Break the Cycle.*

28   Being resilient—able to persevere, even when things are not going as you would like—is a necessary quality for solving complex problems. Perseverance in problem solving has been identified in the new Common Core State Standards (the curriculum that has been adopted by almost all states in the United States) as part of the "Standards of Mathematical Practice" necessary for math success. Resilience has been researched extensively by Carol Dweck as a key to academic and life success. You can learn more about Dweck's work in her book *Mindset: The New Psychology of Success.* Additional practical suggestions can be found in Karen Reivich and Andrew Shatté's book *The Resilience Factor: 7 Keys to Finding Your Inner Strength and Overcoming Life's Hurdles.*

29   Stephen William Hawking is an English theoretical physicist and cosmologist whose scientific books and public appearances have made him an academic celebrity. Hawking has a motor neurone disease that has progressed over the years and has left him almost completely paralyzed.

30   See *A Parent's Guide to Gifted Children*, by James T. Webb, Janet L. Gore, Edward R. Amend, and Arlene R DeVries.

31   Understanding the facts about mental health for any child is extremely important. A parent of a brilliant child must also understand the interplay between high ability and/or asynchronous development and mental health. An excellent resource for parents, educators, and other professionals who work with gifted children (and gifted adults) is *Misdiagnosis and Dual Diagnoses of Gifted Children and Adults* by James T. Webb, Edward R. Amend, Nadia E. Webb, Jean Goerss, Paul Beljan, and F. Richard Olenchak. Another good resource for understanding how a child may be misunderstood and mislabeled, along with remediation strategies, is *The Mislabeled Child* by Brock and Fernette Eide. Eide and Eide also offer a very useful website at www. neurolearning.com. Also, visit the website for SENG (Supporting Emotional Needs of the Gifted) at www.sengifted.org.

32   For more information on selecting a good professional for your brilliant child, visit www.sengifted.org/articles_parenting/Webb_ TipsForSelectingTheRightCounselorForYourGiftedChild.shtml.

33   Robbins & Wilner, 2001

34   See Daniel Pink's fascinating 2010 video on motivation at www.youtube.com/watch?v=u6XAPnuFjJc.

35   McCoach & Siegle, 2003

36   Retrieved from http://bjs.ojp.usdoj.gov/content/glance/cv2.cfm.

37   Retrieved from http://bjs.ojp.usdoj.gov/content/glance/vage.cfm.

38   Finkelhor, Hammer, & Sedlak, 2002

39   Retrieved from http://unh.edu/ccrc.

40   You can find much more information on this topic by looking at the works of Carol Dweck (2006), Daniel Pink (2009) , and Po Bronson and Ashley Merryman (2009).

41   Quinn, 2005

42   If you think any of these tactics sound extreme, you might want to read *Battle Hymn of the Tiger Mother*, by Amy Chua, or visit http://online.wsj.com/article/SB100014240527487041115045760597135 28698754.html for an excerpt.

43   Dweck, 2006

44   Gladwell, 2008

45   National Association for Gifted Children, 2010

46   Loss of the quality of drive is a generational problem, described in detail in Dr. Caffrey's first book, *Drive: 9 Ways to Motivate Your Kids to Succeed.*

47   Piirto, 2004

48   The video *Did You Know?* by Karl Fisch, Scott McLeod, and Jeff Bronman beautifully illustrates the rapidly changing nature of our world. At under five minutes in length, this video is worth seeing. Go to www.youtube.com/watch?v=cL9Wu2kWwSY.

49   Bureau of Labor Statistics, U.S. Department of Labor, 2010

50   Zupek, 2010

51   Webb, 2000

52   Some good ideas can be found in *Cradles of Eminence: Childhoods of More than 700 Famous Men and Women* by Victor and Mildred Goertzel (Goertzel, Goertzel, Goertzel, & Hansen, 2004).

53   Retrieved from www.bigyellowduck.com/people.php?person=BF97F0.

References

Bronson, P., & Merryman, A. (2009). *Nurtureshock: New thinking about children.* New York: Hatchette Book Group.

Bureau of Labor Statistics, U.S. Department of Labor. (2010). *Number of jobs held, labor market activity, and earnings growth among the youngest baby boomers: Results from a longitudinal study.* Retrieved from www.bls.gov/news.release/pdf/nlsoy.pdf

Caffrey, J. (2008). *Drive: 9 ways to motivate your kids to succeed.* Philadelphia: Da Capo Press.

Colangelo, N., & Davis, G. A. (2002). *Handbook of gifted education* (3rd ed.). Boston: Allyn & Bacon.

Coloroso, B. (2008). *The bully, the bullied, and the bystander: From preschool to high school—How parents and teachers can help break the cycle.* New York: HarperCollins.

Coyle, D. (2009). *The talent code: Greatness isn't born. It's grown. Here's how.* New York: Bantam.

Csikszentmihalyi, M. (1990). *Flow: The psychology of optimal experience.* New York: Harper & Row.

Daniels, S., & Piechowski, M. M. (Eds.). (2009). *Living with intensity: Understanding the sensitivity, excitability, and emotional development of gifted children, adolescents, and adults.* Scottsdale, AZ: Great Potential Press.

Dweck, Carol (2006). *Mindset: The New Psychology of Success*. New York: Ballantine Books.

Eide, B., & Eide, F. (2006). *The mislabeled child*. New York: Hyperion.

Ericsson, K. A., Krampe, R. T., & Tesch-Römer, C. (1993). The role of deliberate practice in the acquisition of expert performance. *Psychological Review, 100*(3), 363-406.

Feldman, D. H. (1984). A follow-up of subjects scoring above 180 IQ in Terman's "Genetic Studies of Genius." *Exceptional Children, 50* (6), 518-523.

Finkelhor, D., Hammer, H., & Sedlak, A. J. (2002). *Nonfamily abducted children: National estimates and characteristics*. Retrieved from www. missingkids.com/en_US/documents/nismart2_nonfamily.pdf

Gardner, H. (1983). *Frames of mind: The theory of multiple intelligences*. New York: Basic Books.

Gilman, B. J. (2008). *Academic advocacy for gifted children: A parent's complete guide*. Scottsdale, AZ: Gifted Psychology Press.

Gladwell, M. (2008). *Outliers: The story of success*. New York: Little, Brown.

Goertzel, V., Goertzel, M. G., Goertzel, T. G., & Hansen, A. M. W. (2004). *Cradles of Eminence: Childhoods of more than 700 famous men and women*. Scottsdale, AZ: Great Potential Press.

Gray, A. (n.d.). *Contructivist teaching and learning*. Retrieved from http://saskschoolboards.ca/research/instruction/97-07.htm

Hockenbury, D., & Hockenbury, S. (2011). *Discovering psychology* (5th ed.). New York: Worth.

Levitin, D. (2006). *This is your brain on music: The science of a human obsession*. New York: Dutton/Penguin.

Louv, R. *(2005). Last child in the woods: Saving our children from Nature-Deficit Disorder*. New York: Algonquin Books.

McCoach, D. B., & Siegle, D. (2003). Factors that differentiate under-achieving gifted students from high-achieving gifted students. *Gifted Child Quarterly, 47*, 144-154.

National Association for Gifted Children. (2010). *Redefining giftedness for a new century: Shifting the paradigm.* Retrieved from www.nagc. org/uploadedFiles/About_NAGC/Redefining%20Giftedness%20 for%20a%20New%20Century.pdf

Piirto, J. (2004). *Understanding creativity.* Scottsdale, AZ: Great Potential Press.

Pink, Daniel (2009). *Drive: The surprising truth about what motivates us.* New York: Riverhead Books.

Quinn, M. (2005, Feb. 8). Life of the potty. *San Jose Mercury News,* 1A.

Reivich, R., & Shatté, A. (2002). *The resilience factor: 7 keys to finding your inner strength and overcoming life's hurdles.* New York: Broadway Books.

Renzulli, J. S., & Park, S. (2002). *Giftedness and high school dropouts: Personal, family, and school-related factors* (RM02168). Storrs, CT: The National Research Center on the Gifted and Talented, University of Connecticut.

Rivero, L. (2002). *Creative home schooling: A resource guide for smart families.* Scottsdale, AZ: Great Potential Press.

Rivero, L. (2010). *A parent's guide to gifted teens: Living with intense and creative adolescents.* Scottsdale, AZ: Great Potential Press.

Robbins, A., & Wilner, A. (2001). *Quarterlife crisis: The unique challenges of life in your twenties.* New York: Tarcher/Putnam.

Rogers, K. B. (2002). *Re-forming gifted education. How parents and educators can match the program to the child.* Scottsdale, AZ: Great Potential Press.

Ruf, D. L. (2009). *5 levels of gifted: School issues and educational options.* Scottsdale, AZ: Great Potential Press.

Strip, C. A., & Hirsch, G. (2002). *Helping gifted children soar: A practical guide for parents and teachers.* Scottsdale, AZ: Great Potential Press.

Webb, J. T. (2000). *Do gifted children need special help?* [DVD] Scottsdale, AZ: Great Potential Press.

Webb, J. T. (2009). *Dabrowski's theory and existential depression in gifted children and adults.* Retrieved from www.davidsongifted.org/db/Articles_id_10554.aspx

Webb, J. T., Amend, E. R., Webb, N. E., Goerss, J., Beljan, P., & Olenchak, F. R. (2005). *Misdiagnosis and dual diagnoses of gifted children and adults: ADHD, bipolar, OCD, Asperger's, depression, and other disorders.* Scottsdale, AZ: Great Potential Press.

Webb, J. T., Gore, J. L., Amend, E. R., & DeVries, A. R. (2007). *A parent's guide to gifted children.* Scottsdale, AZ: Great Potential Press.

Winner, E. (1997). *Gifted children: Myths and realities.* New York: Basic Books.

Zupek, R. (2010). *10 careers that didn't exist 10 years ago.* Retrieved from http://jobs.aol.com/articles/2010/01/14/careers-that-didnt-exist-10-years-ago

Index

About the Author

Written by Her Son

Simply put, my mom is an awesome person. While she was raising my sister and me, she taught special education in many different places and led education efforts for AMIkids, a national nonprofit serving at-risk youth. Later, she started a non-public school in Florida called Renaissance Academy, which focuses on the arts. While at Renaissance Academy, she wrote a parenting book called *Drive: 9 Ways to Motivate Your Kids to Achieve*. After my sister and I were grown, she worked for the New York City Department of Education, improving parent involvement and student achievement. You can now find her working as the Superintendent of Schools in Perth Amboy, New Jersey. I could talk about her myriad accomplishments in the world of education and parenting (I think I turned out okay), but it's important that you see the human side of her as well, because someone with lots of accomplishments and no emotions is just a robot—albeit a really smart robot, but a robot nonetheless. Here's a little something you won't find in her normal bio.

When I was little, a couple of robins nested in the wreath on our front door in Audubon, New Jersey. Mom fed them and did everything she could to help them hatch their young once the female laid her eggs. And hatch they did. It was pretty cool having an entire family of birds living on our porch. One day when I came home from preschool, the birds were gone and Mom was crying. You see, a blue jay had come along and lopped off all the little robins' heads with its beak. Apparently blue jays are cruel and do that sort of thing on a regular basis. Mom batted away the jay with a broom, but it was too late. The hatchlings were dead, and their parents had fled. As morbid as this story is, it was a milestone in my life because I saw what an empathetic, caring person my mom is. Plus, she did her motherly duty and taught me about death, never stopping to sugarcoat it or hide it from me. I handed her a pterodactyl eraser I had gotten at the museum to cheer her up. And it did.

To learn more about my mom, go to www.JanineWalkerCaffrey. com.